The Common

Antonio Negri

The Common

Translated by Ed Emery

polity

Copyright © Antonio Negri, 2023

This English edition © Polity Press, 2023

The article 'The Revolution Will Not Be an Explosion Somewhere Down the Road: An Interview with Antonio Negri' by Antonio Negri, Filippo Del Lucchese and Jason E. Smith is reproduced by kind permission of MIT Press. © 2010 by Grey Room, Inc. and the Massachusetts Institute of Technology.

Polity Press
65 Bridge Street
Cambridge CB2 1UR, UK

Polity Press
111 River Street
Hoboken, NJ 07030, USA

All rights reserved. Except for the quotation of short passages for the purpose of criticism and review, no part of this publication may be reproduced, stored in a retrieval system or transmitted, in any form or by any means, electronic, mechanical, photocopying, recording or otherwise, without the prior permission of the publisher.

ISBN-13: 978-1-5095-4426-4- hardback
ISBN-13: 978-1-5095-4427-1- paperback

A catalogue record for this book is available from the British Library.

Library of Congress Control Number: 2022950272

Typeset in 10.5 on 12pt Plantin Std
by Cheshire Typesetting Ltd, Cuddington, Cheshire
Printed and bound in Great Britain by CPI Group (UK) Ltd, Croydon

The publisher has used its best endeavours to ensure that the URLs for external websites referred to in this book are correct and active at the time of going to press. However, the publisher has no responsibility for the websites and can make no guarantee that a site will remain live or that the content is or will remain appropriate.

Every effort has been made to trace all copyright holders, but if any have been overlooked the publisher will be pleased to include any necessary credits in any subsequent reprint or edition.

For further information on Polity, visit our website:
politybooks.com

Contents

Preface: From the Public to the Common   vii

I. Advances
  1. State, Public Spending and the Decrepitude of the Historic Compromise   3
  2. Inside the Crisis: Symptoms of the Common   41

II. The Fundamentals
  3. In Search of *Commonwealth*   55
  4. The Common as a Mode of Production   70
  5. The Law of the Common   81
  6. Federalism and Movements of the Common   92
  7. Disarticulating Ownership? Common Goods and the Possibilities of Law   102

III. Discussions
  8. What Are We Willing to Share? Reflections on a Concept of the Common in the Interregnum We Are Living   115
  9. The Metaphysics of the Common   127
 10. The Revolution Will Not Be an Explosion Somewhere down the Road: An Interview with Antonio Negri   133
 11. On the Institutions of the Common: Prolegomena for a Constituent Inquiry   151

IV. In Conclusion
 12. From the Commune to the Common   165

Notes   179

Preface

From the 'Public' to the 'Common'

Is democracy, as it is interpreted and experienced today in the West, a guarantee of freedom for citizens? The general and generic answer is, more or less, yes. But, as soon as you try to define this 'freedom' and ask yourself what are the effects of its hegemony in the charters of democratic regimes in the West, that consensus vanishes and you get instead confusion and differences of position. This is because that freedom, as embodied in Western democracy, is the freedom of the individual, of the desire to appropriate that defines the individual more than anything else does, of the contract that the individual produces in order to build the collective moment that is necessary for the development of social life. (I use here the term 'collective' rather than 'public' because the latter retains a juridical origin that makes it ill-suited and hardly does justice to the fulness of its usage in social life.)

In the face of growing scepticism, one wonders in fact whether this constitutive process of the collective as a product of individualism responds adequately to the current situation in which citizens live and produce – whether it is capable of bringing about the transformation of individual freedom into the collective freedom that citizens need, in short, whether it can build a civil society free of even greater difficulties and obstacles. As I restate and clarify my position on whether western democracy, in taking individual freedom as its watchword, can be an effective guarantee of a good life for society, my answer has to be in the negative. There is no connection of individual freedoms on a collective terrain, as long as appropriative individuals, together with their contractual prostheses, are held at the centre of society's constitutive process. The appropriative individual, private property, contractual mechanisms and private law are not machines that form a free society; rather they are machines that imprison the desire for sociability and the need to live a good life together – a life that is collectively ordered, a true democracy.

This awareness of society's civil rights crisis and obstacles in the search for freedom itself is ceaselessly renewed in the experience of productive life, which constitutes the backbone of modern society. During the last century of capitalist development, production became increasingly socialized, to the point of crossing a threshold: beyond this point it is no longer the result of a socially invasive process, of alienation and consumption, but has become the collective basis and common foundation of every new order of reproduction in society. We have called this new condition 'postmodernity' – this society where production is completely socialized. The continuous interchange between the private and the collective has reached a point of tendential hegemony of the latter over the former and can be seen in the forms of life that have consolidated in the twenty-first century. And these new forms of life, themselves contradictory, demand to be questioned.

The postmodern order can be described as a heavy (and sometimes horrible) domination exercised by the few over the very many who work, produce and create the wealth of living socially. The transition from modernity to postmodernity, from the industrial mode to the informatics-led and immaterial mode of production, often takes place by preserving the continuity of the old domination. This is due to the inertia of the past or to the ebb and blockage of the new movements of transformation. While life and production have changed, and while the sense of the collective and a thriving socialization have come to a standstill, command remains the same. Representative democracy – which had a hard time portraying values of freedom and participation (and all too often did so deceptively) – is definitively on the decline. The collective has to find means of political expression. This is the only way to save democracy – through self-renewal. But how is that to happen?

In the interregnum in which we were living, it did not take much for a positive 'key' to be introduced in the debate – an element to help us traverse these times and win some space in the conflicts that run through it. (Nothing much was to be expected from those who, like the Marxists who criticized *operaismo*, had come up with proposals for reading the great transition from modernity to postmodernity.) A theoretical key that arose from a reflection on the transformations in the production of life and from perceptions of the advanced degree of its socialization.

Preface: From the Public to the Common

We were sunk in a state of confusion and indistinction. The complete socialization of the form of life gave the sensation of being in a common dark condition. But in order to live one had to turn on a light and shake and question that dead assemblage of lives. We had suffered a becoming common that now confused us. Life rose up and wanted to regain meaning. That 'becoming common' had to be analysed; and immediately it appeared to have two senses. On the one hand, it was a common like a collective of production and consumption in which the domination of capital had been completely realized and that presented itself now in totalitarian form. On the other hand, it was a common that, in addition to the recognition of capitalist socialization, appeared as a capacity of the cooperation of workers and citizens to be effective and as their political power. The maturation of this opposition was the sign of the limits of capitalism in our time; the common showed itself as the active force that recomposed production, society and life into a new experience of freedom.

It may be objected that, at least since the birth of socialism, this trend towards the growing socialization of production has been taken to be a prerequisite of progress towards the common. And the objection is correct. But there are writers, still today, who do not make the distinction but rather emphasize the continuity of eras and see the common as an ideal to be realized across them – one and the same, from the birth of the first workers' leagues to the self-revelation of the worker as a communist in the more advanced informatics networks. This is not true. When we speak of 'the common' today, we do not speak about a utopia to be realized, or an ethical–political principle, or a metaphysical truth that could unite humanity in a project to come. Rather we speak of a being-together, already powerfully realized in daily life, and thus of a real condition (presupposition, foundation) in every form of contemporary life: the common has become the ontological structure of living.

The subject of production, like that of the *polis*, is collective. As such it is organized as labour power and commanded by the order of exploitation. But in this condition, as a subjectivity hitherto objectified, it can – by rebelling, recognizing and assuming the power that constitutes it – break the relationship that binds it to the capitalist order and open up to the order of the common.

The function that keeps these two conditions apart and opposed to each other is private property. The juridical order of property is what constitutes the line of fortification of modern individualism against the postmodern common. And this is an efficacious operation. In this way the common is born in the cage of private property, and when it comes out it is once again caged, put in new chains and in new containers. This is where socialist reformism has done all its misdeeds. But one cannot expect that the power of the common will not explode sooner or later, demolishing all the miserable constraints that hold it back, and that the common will not appear, subjectivated and rearticulated, in institutions that will strengthen, along with freedom, the equality and ability of every citizen to participate in the making of the city.

This book brings together a number of articles, previously not translated into English, in which I continue and deepen at the political level the theoretical work that I conducted with Michael Hardt from 2008 on, in the volume *Commonwealth* (published in 2009), precisely on the subject of the common. As will be seen, my concern in these writings is to ground the concept of the common in a materialist fashion. Only one essay published here, the first, precedes the others: it was written in 1975. But it is useful both because it links the discussion of the common to the Marxist critique of the concept of state (on this account it was part of the political materials produced in the struggles of Italy's long red decade) and because it brings out with clarity, from the beginning, the materiality of the concept of common – which is thus set outside any modernist assimilation to the concept of public. I would therefore say that the pieces in this collection were written against the new metaphysics of the common, against its idealization. We do not know the common as an ideality, except in the hybrid form it takes in financialization – the ultimate expression of the alienated common, the common of money. Or in law. Or – and here we go back to basics – in private property. Each of these aspects of the odyssey of the common is taken into consideration here, as are the steps in a rediscovery of its new materiality: the common as a mode of production – that is, within or against the production of the common: the common as a starting reality from which a new communist project becomes possible.

*

I want to conclude this sixth volume of essays for Polity Press with a few words about Ed Emery – the translator of these trilogies and of many more of my writings. Having come to the end of a life of study and political activity devoted to building a society of free and equal human beings, and having learned how strong the repression of these passions is, the more I feel friendship – or, better, brotherhood – for a man like Ed, who has always been by my side – in sharing intelligence and in overcoming difficulties. Thanks, Ed. In addition I would like to offer a big thank you to Manuela Tecusan for her precious editorial work on these texts.

Part I

Advances

ns

1
State, Public Spending and the Decrepitude of the Historic Compromise*

In this article I continue my exploration of public spending, a discussion that began with my article 'On Some Trends of More Recent Communist Theory of the State: A Critical Review' (now in my volume *Marx in Movement:* Operaismo *in Context* at Polity, 2021).

This is also something of a bibliographic review (many materials not mentioned in the first review, or that have come to my attention subsequently, are presented here). My purpose is simply to set out a proposal for debate.

This deepening of the discussion doesn't come without a polemic – against those who use Marxist terminology to discuss the state but have never read a state budget; against those who philosophize about the state or about the 'autonomy of the political' but do not act in a Marxian way against the concrete modalities of exploitation guaranteed or organized by the state.

1. The problem, broadly outlined: conditions in the literature and conditions in reality

In the major capitalist countries, public spending (of the state and of the public sector) currently approaches or exceeds half of the gross national income. The rate of growth of public spending, as compared with the rate of growth in national income, is an unstoppable

---

* First published as 'Stato, spesa pubblica e fatiscenza del compromesso storico' (1975), in Antonio Negri, *La Forma Stato: Per la critica dell'economia politica della costituzione*, Milan: Feltrinelli, 1977, pp. 233–47 and 251–60.

upward trend.* 'Despite this, in the Marxist literature there are only isolated studies that examine the causes and effects of this unprecedented growth.'[1] And where these studies do exist, only rarely do they capture the specificity of the new situation; rather they find the explanation in the old objectivism of the theory of state monopoly capitalism, with results that are entirely unsatisfactory.

In the theory of state monopoly capitalism, government spending appears as a simple financing of private capital or of its direct public projections. The crisis effects related to the expansion of public spending are both unexplained and inexplicable.

Now, the interpretations of the crisis in the advanced capitalist countries that avoid the problems of public spending, in their indisputable individuality, seem to me rather like Don Ferrante's explanations of the plague!

Yet, while the communist theory of the state has rejected the theses of the theory of state monopoly capitalism and its parallel versions, recently it has not refused to take on board the new relationship between the state (as centre of real and collective attribution of the capitalist ideal) and the critical contortions of the capitalist economy;[2] and there seems to be no doubt now that the state moves as a political and at the same time economic force at the centre of the process of circulation of capital – not a subordinate force but one with essential functions. The trend noted by Marx and Engels is now coming to its completion. And the complementary component of the tendency is also being realized: the action of the working class has a definitely unbalancing effect on the system.

The more the double face of the commodity and of the process of producing commodities is revealed in the antagonism that constitutes them, the more the mechanism of circulation of capital – production plus reproduction – takes place and reaches global proportions in the advanced capitalist state.

But theoretical awareness generally stops here. If the state assumes this central role, as they say, its spending, which means public spending, should be considered as a wage bill of the state as factory [*fabbrica-Stato*].

And when criticism of political economy commits violence against political economy (as communists should), the fight *over* public spending should be seen as a crucial battleground. But no. The statist mythology of the social democratic and revisionist tradition gets

---

* 'upward trend' in English in the original.

the upper hand again and intimidates criticism when it cannot avoid it, or forces it to bow to the capitalist fetishes of balance and financial evaluation! Marx is replaced by Schmidt and Gotha triumphs over critique.

So Jim O'Connor, who has pushed forward the identification of wages and public spending more than anyone else,[3] dithers about the distinction between state as social capital and state as social spending, an analytically useful but entirely abstract distinction, and also a wrong one if it tends to assert that the production and reproduction of elements of variable capital (as is today the chief function of public spending) need to be viewed as unproductive spending. On the contrary, in the second section of Marx's schema for the structure of reproductions,[4] this spending for the reproduction of elements of variable capital is indirectly productive and thus is productive of surplus value, all the more so as the mechanism of capitalist production extends over the whole of society.[5] The gap* that O'Connor rightly registers between directly productive state investments and indirectly productive state spending is not *in itself* a determinant of economic imbalance (as seems implicit in his position): it becomes one insofar as working-class and proletarian action unbalances the relationship in terms of power, of continuous and unrelenting pressure, of continuous struggle.

Even less is it possible to continue to maintain that the crisis induced on state budgets by increased public spending is internal, and indeed determining, in relation to the profitability crisis of mature capitalism.[6] Such a relation no doubt exists, but it is certainly not linear: the crisis does not consist in the increase in public spending, nor does it insist on the fact that this spending is itself in contradiction with private accumulation. Public spending becomes an element of contradiction because working-class and proletarian power upsets the relationship with the state's system of domination – in the capitalist relation the latter is, on the contrary, a balancing element – and upsets it in *the irrationality* of proletarian pressure and workers' struggle.

So then, addressing the relationship between state and public spending means eliminating from the outset any simplification that might derive from objectivisms of the type generated by the theory of state monopolist capitalism. It means assuming once and for all that the state is both terrain and subject of the fundamental contradiction

---

* 'gap' in English in the original.

that capitalist development registers in the face of the social emergence of the proletarian class. It means finally recognizing that the mechanisms of crisis follow, in Marxian fashion, from the 'explosion' (as Marx called it) of the relation that capital is, in other words from the relation between the two classes in struggle, since ultimately everything rests on the 'proportion between necessary labour and surplus value or, if you please,* between the different moments of objectified labour and living labour'[7] around the problem of exploitation and its proportions. Public spending is the public and statal form in which the relationship of statal exploitation of the workers' society of productive labour is misrepresented: public spending is social wage, and the analysis and unbalancing action of the working class must develop on it.

Finally, addressing the relationship between state and public spending means disposing of any residue of social democratic and revisionist statism, of any illusion about the state as a neutral and relatively autonomous mediator, and also of the alleged dual nature of the state – 'good' when it assists private capitalists, 'bad' when it finances them! Unfortunately the state is not Manichean; it is an organic structure of the power of the ruling class. 'Whatever its form, the state is essentially a capitalist machine. State of capitalists, an ideal capitalist collective.'[8] The chapter on the state in *Capital* that Marx did not write was written by the later capitalist development, but it follows the indication left by the Marxian tendency. The duty of critique falls on us.

So much for public spending. A revolutionary use of direct wages, of relative wages, has always been part of the working-class experience: 'the struggle against the reduction of relative wages also means struggle against the commodity character of labour power, that is, against capitalist production as a whole. The fight against the fall in relative wages is no longer a battle carried out on the terrain of mercantile economy but a revolutionary attack on the foundations of this economy; it is the socialist movement of the proletariat.'[9] But a chapter of struggle that remains unknown, or in any case has not reached a sufficient level of militant awareness, is the one that needs to be written on the social wage versus the state.

This is a programme that concerns society's productive labour power in its entirety, at the level of capitalist development that Marx describes as a phase in which the potential of the entire community

---

* 'if you please' in English in the original.

of labour is opposed to capital as a simple mediator of circulation–realization.[10] Here the critique of political economy turns immediately into a critique of politics, because the proletarian assault on the social wage invests public spending as a capitalist terrain of the organization of the relationship between production and consensus, between development and domination, between political constitution and proletarian social struggles.

Here the theoretical practice of capital is a step ahead on a terrain that the proletariat confronts only episodically and spontaneously, when it comes to struggle.

Of course, working-class spontaneity is enormous and deadly: in all mature capitalist countries there is not a single municipal budget that holds – I mean, at the level of the relation of mediation and direct control exercised by the state as employer [*Stato-padrone*]. The capitalist attempt to extort social surplus value in order to mediate and contain the level of social struggles is everywhere in crisis. The mechanism of authorizations and controls – this fundamental key to the administrative rationalization of the state-based command of capital – has been thrown into crisis everywhere, by waves of struggles of appropriation.[11] But even as the levels of working-class struggle are high and strong, capital, too, works continuously on readjustment, on the concentration of control, on administrative planning and spending. Properly speaking, capital and its science do not anticipate the problem but win out on the transition from working-class determination to capitalist closure of the crisis; they anticipate its outcome. 'They' are all working flat out on this. How to close the gap between the state budget and public spending has become the fundamental problem; how to rearticulate together, in one unit, the differences and asymmetries between the mechanism of financial control and the urgencies of political intervention is the second essential problem, correlated to the first.[12] Where the principle of bureaucratic–rational legitimation is insufficiently grounded and incapable of being applied to a too deep and widespread a conflict, one has recourse to charismatic legitimacy, to political pressure, and to participatory mystifications of the 'pink councils' ['*giunte rosa*'], so that the level of inputs* in the demand for public spending be reduced.

But the stakes around these issues are big. Even when the theories of communist writers do not lead us to define the scale of the problem, the behaviour of the two parties in struggle would necessarily

---

* 'inputs' in English in the original.

take us there, anyway: the proletarian insistence in this area, and the capitalist attempt at repressive anticipation. At this point, 'public spending' becomes a central element of the debate. Around it we have to try to understand whether that category includes and transforms some important problems of analysis and of proletarian struggle – namely problems related to the quality and intensity of exploitation – and whether, from the point of view of an overall working-class theoretical practice, the eventual new relations do not modify our assumptions on the definition of the state and the communist struggle against the state.

Of course, an analysis around this theme could be conducted altogether differently; it could be focused on the material dimensions, *chez nous*, of public spending and of the possibilities of working-class attack.

I am aware that many comrades are working on this question, and I hope that the results of their work will soon be made public.

2. An initial analytic approach: elements of evaluation regarding the trend towards the social unification of productive labour

In discussing public spending it is perhaps necessary, more than in any other case, to place oneself firmly on the Marxian ground of analysis of the process of circulation of capital, as a sphere of production and reproduction (and innovation) not only of commodities but also of social relationships, and thus – in the Marxian tendency – of the subject and of revolutionary antagonism. This is difficult when, as happens even in the writers most definitely associated with the class point of view, the neoclassical and Keynesian mystification of the commodity system continues to dominate the horizon.

Take for example the categorization of public spending proposed by J. O'Connor.[13] In his definition, public spending involves the following categories. '(1) Social investments, consisting of projects and services that increase the productivity of given amounts of labour, and, all other factors being stable, increase the rate of profit. This is social constant capital. (2) Social consumption, consisting of projects and services that lower the reproduction costs of labour power and, all other factors being stable, increase the rate of profit. This is variable social capital. (3) Social spending, consisting of projects and services required to maintain social harmony.'[14] Now, this distinction – which is both analytically useful and insecure[15] – becomes dangerous when it is unilaterally assumed to define the gaps* and the reasons for imbalances between sectors of spending. For in this way imbalances, crises, and especially inflation are seen objectively and, to put it in Keynesian language, as arising from dysfunctions in the organization of distribution. But the analysis does not go beyond that tiny barrier. It limits itself without venturing to address the materiality and strength of the social relations that preside over the diversification of sectors and over the disproportions that occur in spending or distribution. 'Necessarily' – as Hirsch notes,[16] when writing about the work of Offe – 'in this way the concept of "society" is reduced to a phenomenological concept of structure' and the state is stripped of the class character which characterizes its (political) structural intervention in society for domination over the relations of reproduction.

Instead, what needs to be immediately attacked is the terrain of the proletarian subject and the location of that subject within the capitalist circulation of goods, because here the changes have been so large as to destroy the possibility of neoclassical and Keynesian interpretations of the asymmetries and imbalances in public spending. In short, my hypothesis is that these are not simply imbalances of distribution; they reveal a much weightier and deeper structure, which is manifest first in the modification of the place and nature of productive labour in mature capitalist society and, second, in the level of struggle and demand for power expressed by the new proletarian subject. I shall attempt to demonstrate this claim.

At the root of the theory of disproportions in public spending and of the theory that inflation is an effect of increase in public spending (especially in the sector that O'Connor defines as 'social spending') lies the belief that 'all or most of state sector jobs are unproductive'.[17] But the possibility that even employees who work in the sector of 'social consumption' (as O'Connor calls it) are non-productive seems definitively excluded by the consideration – already mentioned – that they are subsumed under the second wing of the Marxian schema of reproduction. This leaves the employees of the third group mentioned by O'Connor – the 'social spending' group, which one is imperceptibly led to identify with work in the production of 'luxury' goods – anyway, not producers of value, as one remembers from Marx.[18]

But what does this compartmentalization mean at the present level of capitalist integration (through the state) of civil society? Are the

---

* 'gaps' in English in the original.

workers who contribute to the production of 'social harmony' really unproductive? Or is not rather the concept of productive work that needs to be modified in relation to the Marxian definition,[19] but in the direction of the Marxian tendency? 'The cooperative character of the working process necessarily broadens the concept of productive labour and of its vehicle, that is, of the productive worker. To work productively nowadays, one need not get to work in person; it is enough to be an organ of the collective worker, to carry out some part of its subordinate functions.'[20] In this way the concept would widen its conceptual scope, to match the extension of domination and of the capitalist mode of production.

Now, summing up the results of a long discussion between British Marxist economists on this matter,[21] I. Gough concludes: 'all state workers who produce either components of the real wage, for example social services, or elements of constant capital, for example research and development work, are directly productive for capital', in other words, they produce surplus value.[22]

Bob Rowthorn, for his part, raises the bar and adds that there is no doubt 'that educational and certain other State sectors, although "unproductive", may compel workers to perform surplus labour, some or all of which is transferred to the capitalist sector where it appears as surplus value in the hands of the capitalists'.[23]

In what sense? In the sense that the productive integration of capitalist development increasingly imputes to the state a totalizing function of support with respect to the activity of production. The state does not organize in Keynesian style mercantile relations but productive ones – directly or indirectly, and in any case effectively: productive of goods, and especially of relations of production.

The increase in public spending, its huge growth, is not antagonistic with the development of capital but is organic and necessary to the current, productive figure of capital. Even more, public spending is today the essential prerequisite of every moment of accumulation. Consequently it does not make sense to speak of public spending as being in itself inflationary: at this level of socialization of production and command, the law of value could have an essentially positive test run. If this explodes, if inflationary mechanisms are set into motion unstoppably, that does not depend on the organic relationship that government spending establishes with the composition of capital (over which state command prevails nowadays), but on the break-up of this organic relationship imposed by the working-class and proletarian struggles, on the antagonism that reopens at this point between the organic composition of capital and the political composition of the proletarian class (at this level of unification of labour power which anyway is productive).

The crisis is not in the disproportion between the three forms of spending identified by O'Connor; above all, it does not consist in the contradiction between directly productive and reproductive – hence indirectly productive – spending of labour power on the one hand and, on the other, political state spending, which produces not surplus value but consensus and social harmony. This contradiction does not exist, because consensus and social harmony, if given, are given as functions internal to the relations of direct or indirect production. The crisis consists in capitalism's inability to control the different components that make up capital at this level of class struggle and development of capital; it consists in the irreducibly antagonistic presence of the working class and the proletariat.

But why does collective capital risk extending the crisis from the level of direct production to that of social production? Why does capitalist development involve itself in a dimension that it cannot control directly and in which the problem of public spending (otherwise entirely functional to private capitalization)[24] opens to general contradictions that are relentlessly effective in their social generality?[25] While the precise Marxian definition of the concept of productive labour needs to be modified (and we have seen in what direction),[26] shouldn't there be also a modification of the Marxian analysis of the tendency, one in which the definition and the place of productive labour take another direction as well? This direction consists in allowing the contradiction of the rate of profit to develop. As the individual profit motive declines (for reasons known to anyone who studies the concentration process and the continuous capitalist reform of organic composition in the direction of a greater intensification of constant capital),[27] capital organizes levels of social productivity, steals surplus value from cooperation in production, and replaces the value lost through the permanent and direct assimilation of all the forces of production (and their reduction to constant capital) with the value produced through the general social productivity of proletarian subjects, through the integration of the whole of society into the factory of the collective capitalist.[28] From this point of view, public spending represents the cash flow* of the state as enterpreneur and is played entirely on the structural gap between fall in the rate of profit of enterprises and pressure to increase the general productivity of the

---

* 'cash-flow' in English in the original.

system. The fact that there may be inflationary events within this gap is secondary: the structural gap in public spending does not define its actuality but simply the possibility – a possibility brought about exclusively by the intensity and level of working-class and proletarian struggles.

If all this is true, a number of immediate consequences follow. First of all, public spending manifests itself as a real moment of productive spending, and therefore analysis of it should be entirely correlated with the levels of the circulation of capital in contemporary society. Second, public spending, in its constituting as quantity of money (i.e. means) available to the state for direct or indirect production, weighs as surplus value, extorted from the community of social labour power taken as a whole and from the specificity of the value extracted from social cooperation. Third, it follows that a public spending constituted in this way represents a social exploitation fund for capitalist accumulation and that, as such, it must be both contracted as a wage fund and destroyed as a fund for the financing of capital: and the two moments cannot be split, if Marx's reflections on the relative wage are true.[29] This is, at any rate, a vital terrain of class struggle at this level of development of capitalist exploitation.

It is therefore no coincidence that, in this area, one feels reformist 'theory' pushing heavily forward and pre-emptively defending itself from Marxian critique. As always, here too those in the most intelligent and therefore most dangerous positions regard public spending, correctly, as social surplus value extorted by the collective capitalist.[30]

What follows from this? It follows that, just as the economic expropriation of workers may turn into a political claim of citizens (in the project of the historic compromise, obviously), so, as citizens, they can get their hands on what they were denied as producers! It is clear that the disproportion between the correctness of the analysis and the wretched opportunism of the conclusion can reside only in the author's lack of experience of such propositions.[31] If this were not so – as it is in the far fewer episodic authors of the politics of reformism – we would be dealing here with a shameful ideological mystification and a vile practice of betrayal of the masses.

3. A second analytical approach: on social accumulation, state administration and the contradictions of the capitalist foundation of legitimacy

In the good old days, the enterprise accumulated and the state (preferably a state of right [*stato di diritto*], but it was fine even if it wasn't that) legitimated. Historically, the state as a 'business committee of the bourgeoisie'* has existed as part of capitalist development; and here we need only look at Marx's pages on the use of public debt in the early stages of accumulation and at critical stages of development to prove this more than amply.[32] At this level of capitalist development, to legitimate means grounding the title (on the basis of which an effective and legal relationship is established between the exercise of power and civil consent) in the representative forces of capitalist enterprise, in the values of economic development, and in the directly capitalist mystification of the general interest: the state legitimates inasmuch as it guarantees that the general interest in development is being pursued. At the present level of capitalist development, the situation seems to have changed. A totalizing socialization of capitalist production, rampant processes of abstraction and tertiarization of labour, a general absorption of the so-called forces of production (social cooperation, science, technology and so on) into overall capital, incentivization of the inherence of the infrastructure of social and political services in direct production – all these bring about a structural depth to the state's functions of mediating the process of overall production. Both in terms of organizational functions and in terms of the mass of socially extorted surplus labour, the share due directly to the state has increased enormously. As I have indicated, this process is concurrent with the operation of the law of the tendency of the rate of profit to fall – at the level of the enterprise.[33] The state's accumulation of social surplus value thus appears in the first instance as a compensation for the fall in corporate profits,[34] but in the second instance these new state functions increase in intensity and in determining power: the state begins to present itself as a hegemonic force in the ambit of the capitalist mode of production; the state accumulates in an overriding and determining manner.[35]

---

* This formula appears in Chapter 1 of Karl Marx and Friedrich Engels, *The Communist Manifesto*: 'The executive of the modern state is but a committee for managing the common affairs of the whole bourgeoisie' (https://www.marxists.org/archive/marx/works/1848/communist-manifesto).

How does the principle of legitimacy take form at this level of capitalist development? In the process of general fall in the rate of profit, state accumulation does not make a contribution except in the sense – traditional for countertendency functions – of increasing the mass of profit. This can no longer be a principle of legitimacy: capitalist exploitation has the key feature of tending towards the general interest, in the expectation of development. The mass of profit is not enough to offer legitimacy; it is the rate of profit that, in the capitalist mode of production, gives the power to command and imposes the duty to obey. Now, even if the state of mature capitalism has largely gone beyond the Keynesian functions of regulation of the market, if it has made itself directly productive and if, through quasi-oligopolistic investments in public spending, it tends to achieve regimes of high productivity in the management of services, if the state tries to reorganize the withdrawal of social surplus labour according to a progressive and rational taxation (according to the law of value) – well, even if the state proceeds on this ground, it is far from being able to impose a correct appreciation of the rate of profit.[36] The obstacle is the very nature of social labour in its diffusion and abstractness, that is, in its specific quality at this level of development: the obstacle is that in this case the very possibility of calculation (in relation to the law of value) is, as Marx showed, on the one hand impeded by the spontaneous, value-creating quality of this fact, as for example in cooperation, and on the other outdone when labour time becomes a poor basis for the measurement of the expression of higher capacities of production.[37] Besides, indirectly productive labour, which is the kind of labour largely assigned to the state, yields extremely differentiated and complex possibilities of internal planning.[38] At this point, state intervention in support of the mass of profit is totally 'arbitrary' in terms of the law of value. And there is more: econometric arbitrariness, otherwise fundamental from the point of view of planning overall capital, appears to be totally irrational from a class point of view; and the use of the law of value in this masquerade [*ridotto*] of capitalist resistance is reduced – seems to be reduced, from the proletarian point of view, and that's what counts – to a simple practice of command,[39] all the more if you think that, if capital is essentially a category of relation among class forces in struggle, then the falling rate and the accumulation of mass profit mean, in class terms, a fall in the quota of capital valorization in the face of an implacable massification of proletarian struggles.

So then, on what principle of legitimation – of power and consensus, of discriminating and participatory force, taken together

– can capitalist development direct its movement today? No principle of legitimacy is in the ambit of social state accumulation, this is certain. The state's accumulation of social surplus labour is based on a growing antagonism: capital mystifies this awareness in its own structure and calls the effects of this antagonism a problem of the priorities and selectivity of public intervention.[40] In fact the tax system [*la fiscalità*] is odious. And the exploitation of social cooperation, of indirectly productive labour, of marginalization, of mass scientific innovative capacities – all of this is equally odious. The state's capitalist class understands this situation.[41] So it is that, in this total crisis of credibility, the only moment of real legitimacy is again referred to the principle of enterprise, to the highest level of extortion of surplus labour and production of productivity by the capitalist. The extension of the capitalist mode of production in the form of the state has to subject itself to these levels of productivity as essential moments in the qualification of capitalist reproduction. Regaining high levels of profit (of productivity, of exploitation mystified into profit) becomes a condition and a differentiation of the principle of social development through the state. Here the characteristic situation of the initial phase of capitalist development is overturned: accumulation goes to the state, legitimacy goes to the company [*impresa*]; this drives (in terms of productivity) consensus, the fundamental element of legitimacy of the capitalist state at its most mature level of development. Here the enterprise becomes the carrier [*Träger*] of development in the Marxian sense, its quality and qualification. Productivity as a value-producing element of the social relation of production, this is the legitimating term of the overall process.

Let us return to public spending. If it is one of the figures of the capitalist appropriation of social surplus – perhaps the fundamental one – then it must bend to the norms of productivity of the enterprise. Of course, as we have noted, this is not possible, and for structural reasons. But with this we have not solved the problem. It is within this contradiction that the process offers itself: New York's fiscal crisis in the name of enterprise productivity does not mean that the directly recuperable productive capacities rise to the quantities of accumulation–reproduction of capital; it only indicates that a rule of dominion – repressive, exclusive, terroristic – is reproposed against the uncontainable quality of cooperative, intellectual and innovative labour. At this level of capitalist development, the levels and the quantity of public spending must be statements of authority from the firm, not because this changes the average productivity of the system, locked as it is in the antagonism between the mass of accumulation and of social struggles and the fall in the rate of profit, but because it imposes, reproposes, and legitimately sanctions the rule of capitalist domination.

As always, all the contradictions of capitalist development have a double face. This overturning of the relationship between accumulation and legitimation – in such a manner that the first is attributed to the state, while the second is determined by the enterprise – this overturning of the relationship shows, then, in its working-class aspect, new features and possibilities of proletarian struggle. A huge space of rupture opens for proletarian struggle at the exact moment when the enterprise opens up to the wage in order to ensure productivity and the rate of profit, returning to the state the responsibility to guarantee socially the effectivity of the wage itself and to recover the wage in the social movement of goods. This is the space – the gap* – that exists between the productivity of the enterprise, a project of legitimizing developed capital, and the real terrain of accumulation, a terrain of total social cooperation controlled by the state.

If we wish to deepen and expand the contradiction that this proposal faces at the level of the capitalist plan itself in order to relate it to the antagonism between working-class interests and capitalist development, this can be done in various ways, by lowering company productivity, as the workers have always done, by accentuating the dysfunctions in the social accumulation of the capitalist state, as proletarians spontaneously begin to do...

... Or by doing both together. This seems indeed to be the main line of working-class analysis. In the tendency of labour power to recognize itself as a proletarian unit of insubordinate labour, dualities, ambiguities and crises are innumerable. Working-class analysis dialecticizes and unifies the process, from contradictions within the proletariat to class antagonism.

Now, the factory wage and the social wage are the two poles of the figure in which the working class is mediated and subsumed to the social and state-based figure of capital. Capital tends to separate the two figures, to play the factory wage, treated as an element of legitimacy of the capitalist state, against the emergence of productive unity in social labour; on the contrary, the articulation of the struggle between factory wage and social wage becomes a power that devastates the capitalist contradiction, which is functional to the domination of capital.

---

* 'gap' in English in the original.

But there is one last element to consider; it is not tactical but theoretical this time. In this process, the relative character of the wages contracted by workers explodes. In fact the 'relativity' of the wage contracted by factory workers has to do with the ambiguous relationship, dominated by capital, between the real wage and the monetary wage. Business capital dominates the calculation of the wage at company level, and in the calculation renders it relevant and politically functional. On the other hand, the proletarian struggle over the social wage upsets the capitalist brain and blocks its capacities to calculate and control it. So it appears quite clearly here that it is not at all important whether real wages go up or down: from a Marxian perspective, there can be very few illusions about it! The important thing is to relate the wage component back to the role of independent variable, and this is possible in the action of the proletariat on the social terrain.[42]

Recognizing society as a factory, recognizing the state as a boss, breaking the fetish of productivity as legitimacy and understanding legitimacies in the context of all the needs of the proletariat – today all this is the task of subversion. And this could be enough because, when the relativity of the wage is destroyed, when the causes of division and of domination through division are cancelled out by force, the emperor appears as the children's story powerfully portrays him: naked and mad.

4. The public spending crisis in Italy, restructuring, and the role of the state

The crisis of public finance in Italy in the years after the wave of struggles of the 1960s and the institutional panic that ensued are amply documented[43] and there is a wealth of detailed analysis of these events.[44] How can one summarize them? This is what happened: after 1970, the state's funds and the public administration funds exploded into an overall net deficit, which rose from 2.5 per cent of the national product in that year to 7.9 per cent in 1973. This happened after a strong increase in current spending, which between 1971 and 1973 was progressively higher than that of the national product, and then as a result of insufficient dynamics in tax revenues. Those years saw the steady formation and consolidation of a situation of negative savings, alongside extreme rigidity in capital spending and in transfers in this field. By 1974 the situation changed in appearance rather than in reality, but without any possibility of structural measures, so that there was evidence only of a cyclical action in support of employment, albeit on the basis of a slight improvement. But this support was performed in a minimal and uncoordinated manner, given that the resources continued to be heavily eaten up by the structural deficit.

There is no doubt that during this period public administration was on the ropes as a result of proletarian action and that the levels of exploitation of the social productivity of the system had in consequence been blocked. From a capitalist perspective this situation required an energetic response and a strategy of adjustment was clearly beginning to come into view, although somewhat tentatively. But on what terrain? The terrain was a further step towards the rationalization of circulation, understood as spending restraint and impetus to investment, as well as towards the restoration of global control in all decision-making centres – along with plans for the consolidation of their debt and the reaffirmation of the criterion of legitimacy in public spending. This criterion had to be based on a controlled mediation between deficit* reduction and the definition of a standard† of productivity that matched corporate rules. At a time when the proletariat was discovering the entire social terrain of its exploitation, capital was forced to accept that terrain, but only when the terrain saw the rule of corporate command being reproposed. Break the bad sequences, get your hands on the totality of control, qualify rupture and control in relation to the rule of capitalist enterprise: this is 'good governance' today. And the rethinkings and contortions of science and finance offices are very similar in this respect to those of the scientists and the planning offices, indeed they are assimilated to them.

Let us look at what happens at the level of restructuring intervention: a blockage of spending that comes down to avarice and provocation; total disorganization of the development sequences pathetically conceived of by planning theorists during the past decade;[45] and especially an active policy of stagnation in social labour power and the creation, at this level and in the new proportions and quality of the labour market, of a kind of 'industrial reserve army' in the form of exclusion and parking of entire social layers.[46] In short, restructuring has to bring about the division of the unity of productive labour along internal lines. This labour is potentially revolutionary but in its

---

* 'deficit' in English in the original.
† 'standard' in English in the original.

present condition, through its claim to recognition and to political existence, it is totally destabilizing[47] – to the point where, on the basis of this devastation of the processes of formation of the new political composition of the working class and the proletariat, corporate rule can be effectively reimposed, along with the suffocating legitimacy of the norm of capitalist appropriation of all surplus labour, no matter how it is produced.

And Italy is not an isolated case. Although in other mature capitalist countries the levels of government deficit in relation to the national product are lower than those recorded in Italy,[48] in some of them this deficit is nevertheless substantial; and in any case there is a profound similarity in the readjustment policies and forms of restructuring that are being implemented, because what is being fought is not so much the deficit as the new political class composition that the increased government spending and the eventual deficit register.[49] And in all mature capitalist countries, insofar as the dimensions of the labour market are significant, things are moving around the same project of consolidating social accumulation and legitimizing it in terms of corporate productivity and of mediating the project through measures intended to ruin the struggles of the emerging proletarian subject.[50] This capitalist trend affirms a figure of a highly centralized and functional state; and the norms, behaviours, and procedures that emerge from it concretize the new terrain of legitimacy through the close relationship that joins it to different moments in the process of social accumulation of capital and makes it function. In short, state intervention for the straightening out and orientation of public spending is only a mirror that reflects the consolidation of a principle of legitimacy, not new but exclusive, not previously ineffective but today assumed as a priority efficiency: the principle of corporate productivity on behalf of the social accumulation of capital and against a tendentially unified proletariat, which is expropriated from it.

It is no coincidence, then, that the law – the countersign of the validity of the state's juridical action – must bow more and more to the discriminating materiality of the legitimate action of the state. The formal interpretation and the very formal definition of juridical regulation are increasingly in crisis and give way to functionalist theories,[51] whose most important quality – especially if we don't pay heed to American and German theorists – is insistence on the discriminating criterion of administrative action.[52] Paradoxically from the old juridical point of view, legality can be reconstituted only *ex post*, on the basis of the performance of the substantive functions that are part of the law's ability to direct. It would be possible to develop a rich case history on this subject, but this is not the place. Important here is rather that what is being gradually restored, on the basis of this legal and administrative initiative, is not the old legality but a structure of new rules of behaviour and intervention. In this context, capital and its state tend to make their own the utopian efforts [*conatus*] of all the currents of 'alternative jurisprudence' and to render them effective, demonstrating an open-mindedness unknown to their original mentors.[53]

However, this is only a first step. When the new principle of legitimacy is posited with such heaviness and exclusivity, the lacunas that begin to emerge in local regulations are so common and continuous that even the broad use of evolutive and alternating criteria fails to make it possible to recompose the horizon of traditional legality. Then a very well-known sociopolitical law reappears, with an urgency that always characterizes its functions: intervention becomes exceptional and extraordinary when lacunas in regulation and the urgent nature of the situation require it. In crisis, these functions multiply in frequency and extent: extraordinary administrative interventions, terror-preventing measures, preventive terror, and anticipatory initiatives offer support for and innovation towards evolving, finding alternatives, and fixing new horizons of legality – this time effectively.[54] The formalistic command over the production of new legislation and over the roles of management of the law must unfold from these functional and violent ruptures. After having broken, with devastating intelligence, the old administrative routines, then the principle of legitimacy can permit itself to lie under the same blanket as the new legality.[55]

So let us try to see what capitalist command wants and expects from its functionaries today. It wants to rationalize (i.e. render consequent and continuous) the content of jurisdictional decisions, however and wherever they are proposed, adjusting it to the new principle of legitimacy – in other words to the material discriminant of corporate productivity. The entire complex of social labour is to bend to this imperative: there should be coercive social norms when possible and normative jurisdictional regulatory behaviours in the majority of cases. So then: what remains of the normative systems set up by the working-class and proletarian struggles against the state? Nothing, unless they can be bent to the will of capitalist command, here and now. The Workers' Statute [*Statuto dei lavoratori*] was shipwrecked in Law 300, and the progressive practices of certain sectors of administrative law were perverted into repressive procedures.

What makes law today and determines coherence, certainty and innovation in criminal law is the exceptionality of the (Oronzo) Reale

Decrepitude of the Historic Compromise 21

law. As for jurisdictional and more generally state operators, their job is necessarily one of mediating between the old law and the terroristic innovations in the state system of law: they have to explain rationally the new principle of legitimacy. Rationally and progressively.

If we return to the question of government spending, we need to be aware how fresh the reflections are that its problematic proposes. It's always useful to rediscover a terrain on which the Marxist and working-class thematic of the wage finds further spaces of application: it's useful, first, for showing how the science and practice of capital are constrained to the heaviest of repressive operations for the sake of eliminating the subject that the social wage reveals; second, for finding a terrain of struggle on which all the practices of the hostile power, starting with the social wage, tend to unity from the (massified) point of view of the proletariat; and, third, for determining a further terrain of analysis of working-class hatred.

5. The new proletarian subject in the crisis and restructuring

In a few fundamental pages in the *Grundrisse*, Marx makes various notes on the concept of class composition. As a producer, even the human being, he emphasizes, must be considered, 'from the point of view of the immediate process of production, as production of *fixed capital*', as an accumulation and perfection of capacities of production: gradually the subject that enters into the process of direct production is transformed by it – so that the same process of direct production 'is, as a whole, discipline, if considered in relation to the human who becomes, and exercise, experimental science, materially creative and objectivating science, if considered in relation to the human who has become, whose brain carries the accumulated knowledge of society.' As Marx put it,

> as the bourgeois economic system develops, so does its negation, which constitutes its final result. For now we have to deal again with the process of direct production. If we consider bourgeois society in its broad outlines, as a final result of the social process of production, society itself is always in the picture, or humans themselves, in their social relations. Anything that has a definite form, such as the product and so on, appears only as a moment, a transitory moment, of this movement. The process of direct production appears here only as a moment. The conditions and the objectifications are themselves moments of it in equal measure, and its subjects are only individuals – but individuals in

reciprocal relationships, which they reproduce and also produce *ex novo*. This is their peculiar, unending process of movement, through which they renew both themselves and the world of wealth that they create.[56]

Of interest here is not the philosophical relevance of Marx's materialist definitions, but how to apply his thinking to our present times and stress the specific dialectic between *being moved by* and *moving* capital: this dialectic is based on the emergence of the working class. Because it is here that the new quantity of the wage and the new quality of working-class needs, desires and behaviours are determined, together. And if it is true that in capitalist development the system of needs always takes the form of exchange value and that only utopia can hope to break immediately this alienating relationship, the progressive socialization of labour and its growing abstraction and productivity nevertheless can and must break the specific form of social exploitation. Capital itself moves the class on this terrain, being itself moved there: this is the direction of the extraordinary development of society's productive potential. From this point of view, the more the form of exploitation turns social and the more the form of wage mystification of exploitation turns social too, the more deeply the negation sinks into the body of capitalist society and becomes a determining factor.[57]

Now, moving on to more specific considerations, it seems that behind the expansion of public spending as spending for social wage lie behaviours that suggest a more advanced level of class composition (in the Marxian sense). More and more extensively, in advanced capitalist countries, work* and pay† do not coincide[58] and working-class consciousness more and more extensively accrues levels of salarial presence [*presenza salariale*] that, albeit not organized from a political point of view, are nevertheless unassailable.[59] The process of 'worker education', on which so much revisionist and neo-Gramscian literature has expressed views,[60] has certainly not been left at the mercy of capital and reformism but, reorganized by the struggles, is now structurally rooted in behaviours and needs that only a generalized level of social wage and of political guarantees can now pick up and satisfy.[61] The capital–working-class dialectic, continuously socialized, has brought about a level of political composition of class that characterizes our era in an absolutely new and irreducible manner.

---

* 'work' in English in the original.
† 'pay' in English in the original.

Decrepitude of the Historic Compromise

Yet here the capitalist policy on public spending wants to negate what it shows. As we have seen, it is forced to do so – and without great success, if it is true that, more than managing the containment of levels of income and a marginalizing repression, state action succeeds at most in fanning new relative differentiations, but within permanent levels of guaranteed income. In this, as we shall see again, it plays on the relationship between functions of social accumulation and functions of corporate legitimacy (the mythology of productivity and of 'communist' cooperation against laxity, absenteeism, and... the 'ability to enjoy' discussed by Marx).[62] But the effort to negate the new reality of class composition through a squeeze on public spending is no less effective.

This is all the more so as indirectly productive tertiary sector work, scientific work, and in short all the components of social knowledge come into play on top of the living labour used directly (or momentarily not used in this form). A very extensive literature has now made us aware of the topicality of the Marxian tendency on this terrain.[63] Social knowledge enters with increasing clarity and certainty in the synthesis of the given historical formation: the mechanism of social reproduction tends to make itself scientific in all its fundamental structures, both economic and infrastructural, both informational and political. It is in the continuity of the process of social reproduction of capital that knowledge [*conoscenza*] and knowing [*sapere*], both of them social, become real and progress today. But this accumulation of indirectly productive human activity, this ensemble of living labour that gets exchanged with commodities on the terrain of the production and reproduction of capital, is dominated, divided, differentiated, torn by capitalist command: it is taken on board as a totality from the point of view of exploitation, that is, from the point of view of the realization of the social circulation of exchange values; but it is pushed to the margins of social insignificance insofar as it represents itself as productive labour. Of course, capital, too, may give some conditions for the 'spontaneous' reproduction of this accumulation of social productive labour, but more and more in terms of a 'natural condition' of reproduction whose value is mystified and at the same time greedily sucked into the capitalist recomposition of command (and only of that).[64] The fact is that the opposition, completely objectivistic and reflecting *one* moment in the development of capitalist relations of production, between forces of production and relations of production (where 'forces of production' means science, general social knowledge, quality of work, sociality of work, nature, machinery, organization of work, etc.)[65]... – this opposition was completely resolved in a total subordination of the forces of production to the relations of production and of capitalist command. In this context, public spending is one hundred per cent capitalist spending, investment for capitalist reproduction. The capitalist negation of the creative ensemble of social labour power could not be more thorough. And this is why in the wage dimension, in the sector of the reproduction of social labour power as such, we find the characteristics of the capitalist action on the wage in general: a continuous attempt to reduce necessary labour and a continuous quest for the extraction of the highest mass of social surplus value, pursued with the same greed and monstrous cruelty that we recognize in every factory.

So the struggle for the relative wage opens here, on this ground: it goes from the working-class struggle for the direct wage to the working-class struggle for the social wage. Here, on this ground, fall – even more heavily, if this is possible – a series of traditional divisions of struggle, of economic and political struggle, of union struggle and of struggle for power. But something more is at stake here, on this ground: the response to the working class's urgent call to reappropriate social productivity as against its expropriation by the state, the need to recognize the new subject of production as a revolutionary subject.[66]

This field of struggle opens both as an articulation and as a totality, and from two points of view, that of capitalist command and that of the proletariat. On the first point we must ask, from the working-class point of view, 'whether it is possible that the working class could use the forces of production to valorize itself against capital, as an antagonistic class. Whether an alternative use of highly developed forces of production is possible.'[67] Even more deeply, one might ask whether at this point the concept of class composition, as well as being a descriptive and analytical category, can be translated into an operational category, into an organizational schema of conscious reappropriation of the forces of production to the class.[68] But, as always, these questions have – can only have – a partial answer: this process is under way, but the articulation is meaningful only on the terrain of relations of force in their entirety. This is because the successive appropriation of the forces of production by the class has all the power of capitalist destruction of working-class vanguards and articulations of struggle unleashed against it. Public spending, its ramifications and trends, its planned priorities, and the rationality of command that runs through it are among the key weapons of capital. Public spending brings to social accumulation and to workers' social struggle a legitimation of the capitalist enterprise that is based on the rate of profit, the state guarantee of an accumulation for profit. Public spending organizes the community of labour so as to destroy a possible political form and to subject it entirely to the legitimacy of the rate of profit; a new working-class world capable of communism has to bend to the dead fetish of a falling rate of profit.

Thus the effects of state action against the revolutionary recomposition of the new subject of production can be counteracted only on the terrain of totality. The only thing that can address the legitimacy of the restructured capitalist state is the living collective legitimation of a communist reappropriation of the forces of production by the proletariat, by that independent force of production that is living labour. And when the legitimacy of the capitalist state is, of necessity, articulated on terror and on power to devastate the working class, only the power [*potere*] struggle – power against power, terror against terror – gives the working class and the proletarian struggle dignity. The whole capitalist restructuring is bent on the project of destroying the new composition of social productive labour and its political potential. The whole institutional restructuring is just as coherently oriented towards mediating between old formal assertions of legality and new emergent functional needs as to be effective anyhow. The normative soul of these rules of capitalist restructuring is the law of the falling rate of profit, an awareness (to echo Marx) that tolls the death knell for the civilization of capital. Here the tension between the state and the new proletarian subject cannot but be destructive. But while on the capitalist side everything is short term and the will to destroy stinks of pessimism and delusion, on the workers' side the will to destroy is terrible, because it is sustained by the hope and certainty that in the long run we shall all live. Today the analysis of power from the class point of view is less and less interesting. Fundamental is instead that we pay attention to the behaviours of the new proletarian subject, in other words to the permanent illegality of this subject's daily actions, and that we pay attention to the analysis of power only afterwards, as the 'reply' of the employing class.

6. More on the functions of accumulation and legitimation of public spending

Planning is done by big business for big business:* this is not true today, just as it was not true yesterday. Neither *économie concertée*

---

* 'Planning is done by big business for big business' in English in the original.

['concerted economy'] nor the various forms of mixed economy* have ever been reduced to this. The fact that enterprise logic dominates and legitimates the processes of planning does not mean that these were ever simple projections of an immediate interest of big capital. Planning is rather to mediate between social forces, to determine the materiality of the infrastructures of production, to incentivize the overall productivity of the system, to ascribe centrally, to the power of the state, the power – active or passive – to organize the social circulation of commodities. Public spending is the cost of these overall operations and, as a feature of the wage aspect of state activity in the field of programming, it certainly cannot be just subsumed to the will of big capital.[69] Planning means above all to repropose, through organizational mediation, a terrain for the composition of class conflicts – once it is established that, at these levels of class struggle, the dual development intrinsic to the capitalist logic of domination is completely affirmed.[70]

And yet all this was... once upon a time! There was a reformist hope that the conflicts could be mediated in reality and that the reorganization of the labour market by mediating between productive functions of a social nature and welfare† could be sustained within foreseeable and controllable proportions. In fact there is no highly developed capitalist country that has not experienced the crisis of this project. The economic potential of the new proletarian subject has got embroiled in the project of planning, and even if it has not managed to appear as continuous struggle, it has nevertheless appeared as qualitative and quantitative insubordination at the level of the wage. Keynesianism, the Keynesian utopia, and the alternative utopia of the Keynesian left are all burned out on this side of the class struggle.[71] On this point, social accumulation and corporate legitimacy are mutually hostile: public spending finances social struggles rather than the mediation between social accumulation and corporate legitimacy.

It is at this point that capital translates crisis into restructuring, or rather plays the former for the latter on the basis of these assumptions. The fundamental element of capitalist strategy consists in shattering the link between social accumulation and legitimation and therefore in transforming public spending into a schema of devastation (when possible; otherwise of containment) of the massive presence of the proletariat in society and of incentivization of models of produc-

---

* 'mixed economy' in English in the original.
† 'welfare' in English in the original.

tion matched to the profit rates required. The project is to block the increase of the cost of social labour and to exploit it across the board without paying for it – or rather by paying simply for the expenses of a 'natural' reproduction of social labour, by compressing necessary social labour and by increasing surplus social labour. At this point public spending – an incentivized sort extraordinarily expanded on the basis of a class pressure together with the capitalist recognition of the essential character of general social labouring – itself breaks its ambiguity: it gradually has to become an expression not of value theory but of its capitalist destruction; it must be a current element in the capitalist practice of command.

Let us return more concretely to the basic terms of the discussion. This means taking the discourse to the highest level of abstraction. It means showing that essential dialectical transition that is the working-class (and capitalist) overcoming of the barrier of the law of value when – in fact at the very moment in which – it is realized.[72] Historically, the socialization of productive labour and the complete domination of society by the law of value bring into being a complex of statal activities that negate the spontaneous valence of the law of value: and this happens in 'socialist'[73] as well as in highly developed capitalist societies.[74] In both, the operation of the law of value is given only under the state's 'enforced control':* we call this 'bureaucratization' in socialist societies and 'authoritarianism' in capitalist societies, and the result is the same. Nor are 'Weberian' illusions permitted – as if the introduction of a charismatic innovation could fluidify the functioning of the law of value and guarantee the plan. The fact is that, in the dialectic between relations of production and forces of production, the law of value acts as a fundamental term in the organization of exploitation; its realization realizes exploitation and brings about the onset of absolutely particular conditions of insurgence – that is, conditions such that the spontaneity of the operation of the law has to be heavily corrected, because it is not a definitive production asset but a blockage to the expansion of the force of production that its self-realization brings about. At this point, then, only command, without the plausibility of the self-expression of social labour, represents the validity of the law of value, whereas all the action of the new proletarian subject spontaneously expresses intolerance of and rebellion against this barrier that is set up against the force of production.

---

* 'enforced control' in English in the original.

Capital and its collective brain know all this, and act accordingly. It is here that public spending reforms itself into the repressive irrationality of capitalist command. But here, too, the critique of political economy, having been emptied out through the draining of the law of value, leaves room for the critique of politics *tout court*: not a critique of politics that simply addresses the political forces but one that confronts especially the problem of command and of its institutional organization, which is functional to social production. And here it is possible to show the functional and structural contradictions that the fall of the law of value and the replacement of market calculation[75] with the political law of the plan (of restructuring) open for working-class struggle.

This is where the problematic of public spending becomes a terrain of working-class critique inasmuch as the struggle over the relative social wage can be immediately functional to the deepening of institutional contradictions and to the struggle against the institutions. Critique of political economy versus critique of politics versus critique of administration, of planning, of restructuring: this is the path we are taking.

On the other hand, all the determinations of state action against the working class – determinations that take place in the specific context of restructuring but already qualify as medium-term trends – converge on this point: to destroy any illusion of planning as far as the realization of the law of value is concerned and, on the contrary, to act along internal lines towards the devastation of the unitary potential of the proletariat as a productive and revolutionary force. Public spending must essentially guarantee a process of arbitrary segmentation of labour power, destroying any relationship between production and qualification,[76] any value-making sequence between overall social formation [*formazione*] and production value, and bringing about not so much a split between the employed labour force and the industrial reserve army[77] as a fierce split between the various layers of labour power that stand at oppose ends of the wages spectrum.[78] Overall rigidity in public spending – a point now conceded – must be rearticulated here according to the schemas of command or restructuring, not so much with a view to recovering profits as for the sake of the ongoing existence of the capitalist mode of production.

This is a situation in which any reformist operation, however conceived, runs out of credibility in the space of a morning. In effect no room is left here to set the state in contradiction with the objectives of the working class concerning the social wage: this space was

Decrepitude of the Historic Compromise 29

burned when public spending was entirely subsumed to the criterion of corporate legitimation. Every case of reform shows as its outcome the capitalist attack on working-class socialization, the attempt to devastate the social form of production. All the dysfunctions and disarticulations of the administration, in which reformist action gets more and more dramatically mired, are defined not on an abstract, rational terrain but on a functional one – insofar as it is determined by specific structural needs, and these are exclusively determined in their turn by the relations fixed by the class struggle.[79] Administrative action is decisively irrational, since its rationality cannot reside in the social functioning of the law of value but simply in the practical power [*potenza*] of capitalist command. Here administrative rationality does not become terror, it *is* terror. Remove from capitalist society its only rationality, which is the one founded on the greed of exploitation, and you will have this baroque monster of provocation and devastation.

Restructuring does not resolve the capitalist crisis; it accentuates it. The analysis of public spending shows this in the clearest form. This is, then, the relationship that does not hold: the relationship between the need to respond in some way to the salarial demands of a more and more massive social labour power – between the urgent need to collect the processes of social accumulation under salarial form – and the rule of capitalist profitability; in other words between the fall of the historical barrier of the law of value and the capitalist determination to enforce the law of value at all costs, in fixed proportions. It is within this contradictory relationship that public spending is placed. It doesn't matter how shaky are the supports that reformism can offer. There are fewer and fewer possibilities of mediation between these two terms: between the emergence of a new mode of production, internalized to a new working-class and proletarian composition, and the enforced* permanence of the capitalist rule of command.

The crisis of public spending should be privileged in our analysis because it presents together both the positive (workers, collectives) and the negative factors (the bosses' command) of the general crisis. But it is clear that here the analysis of the crisis brings us back directly to the figure of the state, to the collapse of its dignity as a mediator of capitalist production. The Marxian paradox is realized in this case, too: the more the state resolves civil society and the power to com-

---

* 'enforced' in English in the original.

mand social production fully by itself and the more this resolution looks dialectically uncertain, the more the working class demonstrates its real hegemony over society. The revolutionary project of communism lives this contradiction and this possibility.

7. The historic compromise: ideological decrepitude and repressive actuality

Insofar as it is an institutional movement, the labour movement appears today to be revisionist in ideology, reformist in project and technocratic in practice. Let us examine the effects of this situation point by point.

The ideological revisionism of the institutional labour movement has a long history in Italy. In some respects this history sees itself as Gramscian. In fact the concept of hegemony in and over civil society is strongly innovative in relation to Marxist–Leninist paradigms of the conception of the state.[80] First and foremost, there is a space of ideological mediation for this concept, a space to be entrusted to the social power of the labour movement as the precondition of a revolutionary process that attacks the social forces of production, according to models of overall adhesion. All this has a dignity that revisionism, which affects the proposal, cannot negate; and it also corresponds to a given stage (the pre-fascist stage) in the development of the forces of production in Italy, and consequently reproposes itself as a response to the need for political antifascist action. So it is not the revisionism of the Gramscian proposal that renders the thematic of the institutional labour movement ideologically dangerous; rather it is the present-day use of formulas that are more or less Gramscian in origin. The proposal of hegemony requires a definition of civil society. But today civil society is dead; it has been subsumed to capitalist development and reshaped by the social unity of productive labour. In this situation, a hegemonic process is completely subordinated to the solid imperative of capital's social command on profit, a command that reorganizes civil society and causes it to exist only as a projection of the process of production and of the structures of power. Conceptions of alliances, policies manoeuvred in the mixed economy, and ideological pressure on the middle classes, all unfold on the crumbling image of civil society, whereas the reality of class struggle shows instead continuity on the terrain of insubordination and a tendential unification of proletarian subjects in the struggle against the state.

On the other hand, what remains of the discourse concerning institutional relations and mediations, a discourse proposed by revisionism that is necessary and complementary to the discussion of tactics? What remains of the discourse concerning the continuity of the democratic struggle and of the struggle for socialism? And what remains of the predisposition of existing constitutional structures to support this continuity of struggle? The framework of relations, not only social but also institutional ones, has so much fallen apart in the crisis of the late capitalist state that the terrain of constitutional reality is necessarily transcended and overturned by the power of the bourgeoisie, the fundamental principles of democratic coexistence are selected with a view to consensus, and the problem of consensus is systematically resolved according to an anticipated tendency to certain types of behaviour, be they authoritarian or terrorist. Today more than ever, the framework of legitimacy, the sources of authority, the very process of material validation of power are placed so much outside of the schema of democratic legitimation that, as Luxemburg predicted, radical democratic struggle, far from being a first stage, becomes the foundation of working-class struggle.

The fact is that socialism becomes impossible at the moment when the working-class struggle causes a definitive crisis in the functioning of the law of value – not only in the sense that through its action it determines and strengthens the functioning of the tendential law of the falling rate of profit but also in the sense, which goes even deeper, that it throws out of balance the very terms on which the law operated, removing that sense of a relationship between necessary labour and surplus value on which ultimately everything is based. Socialism, all the utopias of socialism, would like to represent the actualized reality of the law of value, its realization, which is like saying the complete real subsumption of the social labour of capital. But this is possible only in relation to a dialectic of the classes, only as a moment of class struggle. At this point all the variants of the socialist utopia, both objectivist (socialism as socialization of the means of production and as rationality of command) and subjectivist (a new way of doing production, cooperation, participation, co-management and so on), sink into crisis, because the law of value is not realized except by splitting itself – by imposing, at a very high level, the new antagonism between capitalist labour and command, no matter how legitimated, and the totality of the social productive force of the proletariat.

The decrepitude of the reformist model, linked as it is to the ideology of the planned realization of the law of value, becomes even more apparent at this point. One need only look again at the problematic of public spending, at how it sets itself in the perspective of reformism, and at the new antagonisms to which the reformist option will give space. Reformists see public spending as an expense, productive both directly and indirectly. They tend, rightly, to rationalize its management, to bend it to the rigidity of the schema of priorities, to guide development through it, and to influence its direction. But, as we have seen, beyond these formal criteria there is a contradiction between the form of social accumulation and the source – measure, proportion – of its legitimacy, a class contradiction that reveals the tendential unification of the social and productive subject and *thereby* the irrationality of the proposed criterion of corporate legitimation. Subjectivizing itself in terms of class, the contradiction becomes explosive. The pressure on public spending turns in fact into wage pressure, the political struggle of the working class for the relative wage and (especially and specifically in our times) against capitalist work – a working-class allusion to the newly emerged force of production, which wants to be paid in this capacity.

In this tangle of contradictions, the attempt to rationalize public spending becomes immediately repressive: such rationalization necessarily has to follow corporate parameters and to explicate the corporate figure of the state. It becomes repressive not so much because it uses for this purpose the tools of the repressive power of the state and of all its multiplying separate bodies [*corpi separati*], but because it uses them within the intensity of an unresolvable structural contradiction. If socialism is impossible, then reformism is all the more so. Any reformist action is immediately repressive.[81]

Here it begins to be apparent that the revisionism and the reformism of the official labour movement are subject not only to the repercussions of the decrepitude of the conception of class relations that underlies them. The unreasonable nature of their project fuels an unreasonable will, which is intent on the realization of the old design no matter the cost. The support that communist reformism gives to the project of capitalist restructuring derives from the need to repress forcefully a proletarian subject that has achieved unity, exerts pressure on the state budget, demands payment for the social labour extorted from itself, and also presses against the barriers of an order that has been established for the purpose of legitimizing the imperial rule of corporate profits across all aspects of social cooperation. Actively repressing the proletarian front, restructuring the social subject of production, segmenting the markets of labour power, guaranteeing mobility processes that destroy working-class power and achieving a terroristic marginalization of entire social strata: these operations become both the foundation and the content of reformism, in Italy as in all capitalist countries under social democratic management. Here is the content of the 'first phase' of reformism, which perpetuates itself everywhere as the base of the determination to repropose an impossible socialism! The decrepitude of the ideological project is here totally indistinguishable from the repressive actuality of the action of reformism.

Hence we get those operations of class division, especially in the sector of productive intelligence – which, by socializing and tertiarizing itself, has begun to represent the true connective tissue and the central nervous system of the processes of social accumulation of capital, as we have seen. For capitalists, it is fundamental to deny and conceal especially the class nature of these new roles and sectors, to mystify their functions by falling back on the old trope of the 'middle classes'. Fundamental, but not painless, because these directly social functions of the force of production perceive themselves to be less and less *socially* legitimated; rather they feel more and more strongly how the *authoritarian* legitimation of their role is imposed on them. The proposal, which is imposed on them, is that they be the bearers [*Träger*] of the bureaucratic and terroristic mediation of a socialism with an authoritarian face, of a productive rationality that reproduces the dead logic of corporations, mystifies the social density of the process of accumulation, and negates the very nature of productive work, subjecting it to the parameters of command, of a subordinated and subordinating function. The roles of state administration are increasingly caught up in this contradiction, which they themselves create, all the more so as in this situation the crisis of reformism must be contained. The technocratic figure that is increasingly attributed to these roles is, subjectively, in crisis the more the functionality of their rationalizing action appears to be directly terroristic.

In Italy, the historic compromise represents entirely a figure of the advanced form of the social democratic state for the management of the capitalist crisis. The entry, of undoubted historical importance, of Italian communism (and probably of all the communist parties of the Latin Mediterranean area) into the power block of European social democracy changes all the political terms of the class struggle. As for the figure of the state, we have begun to see the sense in which it is increasingly defined by the urgencies of command.

The point of intersection between the development of reformism and the structure of the state has probably been reached already. From now on, the class point of view must retain this new political synthesis: here is finally the enemy to be fought, and over a long period.

8. An old tactic for a new strategy

Let us return to public spending. Why did I choose this topos to demarcate a terrain for general discussion? Because the analysis of the objective contradictions into which capitalist restructuring and the state of reformism are forced can transform the question of public spending into a subjective terrain – potentially it is that: it is the terrain of the wage struggle, with all the political implications that, in true Luxemburg spirit, should be attributed to the struggle over the relative wage. Public spending amounts to being on the one hand a social production terrain and on the other a social wage terrain. In short, it is an aspect, always more relevant, of the self-expression of social capital in its internal dialectic. This means that dealing with public spending is equivalent to raising the problem of working-class antagonism in the relationship between society and the state. It indicates a form of capitalist subsumption of labour and at the same time the fabric on which the antagonism can subjectively be determined.

It is therefore not enough to highlight – as does Alfred Sohn-Rethel (and very well, too) in a recent essay[82] – the opposition that opens up now, in the society of mature capitalism, between the accomplished structure of the relations of domination for exploitation and the working-class society that creates, continuously and completely, the totality of social wealth – or between a formed economy [Lat. *economia formata*] and an economy in formation [Lat. *economia formans*]. Nor is it enough to highlight the enormous progress of social industriousness [*laborosità*], directly and indirectly productive, and to set it against the process of social accumulation, which lies firmly in capitalist hands. Marx had already seen all this, and with great lucidity: 'These are pages,' comments Rosdolsky in speaking of what he takes from the *Grundrisse* on this point, 'that (albeit written more than a century ago) can only be read with bated breath, because they contain one of the most daring visions of the human mind.'[83] The end of the material barrier of the law of value, automation of the force of production, and the liberation of invention power: Marx sees, describes and projects on all this, as a direct and material precondition for the building of communism.

But this is not enough: here subjectivity is, must be, cannot but be the keystone of the process. Within the possibility of communism there is an enormous set of needs and desires that begin to liberate themselves. We, individually, can have only 'rough' prefigurations – adds Marx[84] – the only prefiguration that we can operate collectively is given through struggle. Taking on a terrain of struggle is not to exhaust the totality, it cannot be that; nor can it allude to a significative set of realized needs. Assuming the struggle is, in the first place, to assume the negativity of the need for destruction. The wage is a terrain of struggle that, reproposed at this level, can in principle explode the entire potential of needs, the Saint Barbara of desires. And then, only at this point, quantity passes into quality (in Marxian jargon) and innovation, project, and an eager desire are unleashed. Our task cannot be to prophesy the future; it is to identify the contradiction on which the future is being realized, in a dimension and with an intensity that no individual can master, but that the masses know how to produce. Thus the slogan 'social wage against the state' is not a strategy but the practical identification of a terrain of struggle. Such identification starts from the determination of the contradictions that reformism and power cannot resolve and is carried out in the theoretical certainty that today any open and conscious class struggle is immediately and necessarily a struggle for communism. In the field of public spending, the old tactic of struggle over the relative wage opens the proposal that the strategy of communism needs. Today any mass space built through struggle can be only a breach from which arises the mass of desires that are contained and repressed by the social mode of production for capitalist accumulation. We can see in everyday life how many and how intense these desires are, and how impatient and communicative their force of expression is. All this is due to the very form of capitalist production, to the socialization of exploitation, to the heaviness and totality of the process of capitalist irrationalization of social relationships; but it is also due to resistance and awareness of the complexity of exploitation, both of which are now present among the great mass of workers. The wage is the category with the help of which capital collects and mystifies, in basic form, the complex of political and social, historical and human expectations of the proletariat. Today capital has been forced to collect the wage, or a large part of it, in the form of public spending, and this is the first place where contradictions can explode: social wage against the state.

A number of elements show that contradictions are already exploding, in a new form. Resistance to the expropriation of the surplus value of social production is no longer exercised in the simple old forms of trade union defence, directly implanted in large factories;

it finds new forms of propaganda and attack by immediately tackling the social levels of accumulation. The forms of the struggle for self-reduction* are first and foremost an expansion of the working-class wage struggle.

But not only that. Gradually, as class consciousness grows, awareness of the new terrain of struggle grows too, at the general social level. The working-class reappropriation of working time and time of freedom, which has always developed in factories, takes place today within the struggle for social reappropriation, for the social wage. Self-reduction is the latest, highest form of the struggle of the mass worker and the first figure in which the social reappropriation of wealth takes place in the name of the new proletarian subject of the class struggle: negation and sublimation of the mass worker.

The transitions from the dialectic of class composition are given here in a subjective form. Resistance, self-reduction, appropriation: these forms of struggle follow the same path as the transformation of class composition. The terrain is, without doubt or hesitation, that of the social wage. The political will is to exacerbate the contradictions that capitalist leadership is experiencing on that terrain. The forms of struggle progress in succession: the second struggle transforms the limits of the first into points of attack, and the third does the same to the second. Within these qualitative transitions the composition of the proletariat is transformed into reality and expands as political consciousness and will. Wealth becomes palpable; class consciousness turns its engine into an objective of its own and with this solves the bad features of a dialectic that otherwise is always unfinished and inconclusive. Mediation and immediateness get closer to each other when the material terrain of the mediations of consciousness is expressed in the direct recuperation of wealth and power.

All this applies extensively, in line with the growth of the social worker, with the overturning of capitalist socialization and its transformation into a social recomposition of the proletariat, and with the subjectivation of abstract labour. But there are also a number of examples related to the progress of the communist struggle over the social wage in large factories, in the middle of the most active and conscious proletarian struggles. Here the relationship between social power of production and capitalist command runs along the organization of labour and the structure of fixed capital. Now, in this

---

* Self-reduction [*autoriduzione*] of prices is a practice of refusing to comply with price increases and a movement of reducing and controlling them collectively.

situation too, during the latest struggles, in the strikes in reverse,* the collective will for reappropriation has been able to express itself as *potere*. Taking over workplaces and putting them back into operation, not to produce but to test positively the class's associative productive *potenza* to prepare the best possibilities for sabotage and struggle in the immediate future – this is what has been done. Working-class consciousness has not produced a prefiguration but has focused on its own collective and mass deepening in order to define a further path of struggle. The will for reappropriation realizes, at the social level and at the level of the factory, the working-class tendency towards communism to the extent that it liquidates, in mass action, the implacably hostile power of the socialist mediation of the relations of social domination. When individual episodes rise to the level of appropriation, the struggle for the social wage reveals the working-class tendency to transform the use of the specific new contradictions of the capitalist mechanism of social accumulation into a struggle over power, a struggle for communism.

Another element of extreme importance as regards the political and structural contradictions of public spending derives from the analysis of the state and of the administrative roles of its management. In other words it derives from a deepening of the critique of the political economy of administration.[85] If it is true, as I have pointed out many times, that the role of the state becomes more and more structural and internal to the development of accumulation, we shall have to see what are the contradictions to which the state-administrative roles of social capital are subjected. Now, on the one hand, the fact that these roles become immediately productive is already demonstrated, paradoxically, by the heavy pressure on them for productive action – for an always more rationally productive action. Simple bureaucratic rationalization? It doesn't look like it: here the functionality becomes indirectly productive – productive in the proper sense, of surplus value – because through the functionality of the administration the processes of social accumulation are connected to the processes of corporate legitimation. The role of employees in the administration becomes at this point immediately contradictory: on the one hand they are a moment in the social labour process, on the other they are called to manage it for the sake

---

* A reverse strike, *un sciopero alla rovescia*, is 'a unionist form of protest around the execution of work not requested or forbidden by the employer' (https://www.diatomea.net).

of profit. The increase in the productivity of public administration means in the last resort that this contradictoriness is solved in totally capitalist terms of efficiency. But the contradiction is big. At one end, awareness of being a participant in the social fabric of production extends even further, being driven by the very improvement of the machinery of the state; at the other end, the general absence of reasonableness in capitalist command over the state apparatus induces logics of crisis and sometimes of effective insubordination. Of course, the ideology of participation, of technocracy, of reformist and bureaucratic socialism has a far from insignificant impact on these social elements. Perhaps this is not yet decisive, but they are likely to be confronted and defeated on the basis of a further, broad progression of the contradictions and antagonisms of capitalist socialization. In any case they are susceptible to being contested and opposed and, in some cases, reversed by the action of agitation and proletarian organization.

In what sense? To speak of reappropriation in this instance, too, is meaningless; it would be to indulge in notions of an alternative, in the illusion of an alternative in the command of the state! What must be conquered at this level is rather an awareness of the participation of some of the people who fulfil administrative roles in the social community of working-class production – and therefore an awareness of the possibilities of struggle that may exist even in the enemy's territory. To be a sniper, an informant on the movements of the enemy, a provocateur: this is the only alternative that class consciousness can introduce among the roles of productive administration from above and can oppose to the socialist utopia of alternative uses of state command, with its delirious proposal for a 'revolution from above' – a frantic last mystification of 'salami theory' (taking power in slices) of the classical social democratic tradition.

'The strategic dimension of refusal and the tactical dimension of abnormal usages' (as the slogan goes) need to be offered here as a terrain of class struggle in administration; and they are possible if this type of struggle is part of being aware that the administrative role often becomes a specifically productive role – productive indirectly, yes, but still productive of surplus value.[86]

When it comes to the roles of the productive administration of the state, is there not a function more directly connected to the complexity of the social proletarian form of production and of the production of struggle? Is not a purely negative and destructive indication of tasks implicitly inconsistent with social labour's definition of some of these roles? These doubts and these questions require deeper research and, above all, a documented basis of behaviours and struggles, in order to produce a different answer from the one given thus far. What is certain is that, whatever tendency the struggles in these sectors will reveal, the only fixed point of analysis will be an extension rather than a negation of what has been said. And it is not impossible that, with the extension of the behaviours of refusal, there will also be qualitative leaps in the struggles of administrative personnel in the state. But, until we reach that point, the Leninist teaching on the hostile nature of the capitalist state remains perfectly complementary to the development of the Marxian tendency of integrating the state and the global ideal capitalist.

The only certain thing that one can add is that the potential for destruction, for a struggle against capital carried out by some roles in the productive administration of the state, is revealed by the critique of the political economy of administration to be extremely high and strong. It is therefore no coincidence that reformism's will to be integrated today turns again with such vigour to the capture of the middle classes, mostly in a desire to repress a class identification that was certainly happening in the most recent phase of struggle.

Last but not least:* starting from the consideration of public spending, one can begin to unify tactical indications and lines of strategy for the struggle, and above all one can begin to relaunch an analysis of political class composition, paying particular attention to the new layers, which are invested simultaneously by the socialization of the mode of production and by the proletarianization of their conditions of life and struggle. As public spending policy extends as a system of social control, on the one hand it invests new social sectors, potentially taking them towards a clash with the state, and on the other it introduces class contradictions in the machinery of the state, among the operators of state administration. Seeing this clearly and proceeding far more analytically than could have been done here, both in research and in unrest, can lead to significant innovations in the science of social class. The Marxist terms of a possible discussion are more or less given. But the creative intensification of research is still to happen. It is necessary to ascribe the continuation of this discussion to the subjects of administration themselves, to the comrades who work there and are subjected to exploitation, but who also transmit capitalist command. This should be done for an analysis of the state, for a critique of politics and administration, for a new

---

* 'Last but not least' in English in the original.

step forward in the analysis of political class composition at this level of the development of the forces of production – and against the reformist conception of power, of the state, and of the roles of administration.

2
Inside the Crisis

Symptoms of the Common[*]

In a philosophical debate a while ago I had occasion to comment on an observation made by Hannah Arendt: the treasure of the freedom of action is impossible to transmit in a world that does not attribute meaning to acting in public. Now, while I was preparing the present article, this observation sprang to my mind as an opportunity for discussion. If taken positively, it tells us that we are free only if we live a common experience, in other words if we succeed in achieving a space–time in which freedom can not only express itself but also become concrete, and action [*l'agire*] is able not only to expand but also to make itself an institution.

But there are at least two terms in this observation of Arendt's that need to be underlined: 'transmit' and 'public'. When we say 'transmit', our meaning is customary and clear; there is a deposit and a passage, an accumulation and a common enrichment, a subjectivity from which a lived experience, or a language, can be passed on to someone else. *But today, in the economic and social crisis that we inhabit, what would this mean, for instance to the younger generations, which do not have a future and are struggling in a situation of uncertainty and danger?* When we then pick up the term 'public', this brings us to a really difficult aspect of our present times: the difficulty we have in using this term, as Arendt points out, is that the concept of public has probably detached itself from the meaning it once had in our tradition, in which the passage from the private to the public was

---

[*] From the lecture 'Vivre dans la crise', delivered at the Centre for Art and Media, Karlsruhe, 13 June 2013. This is the translation of an unpublished Italian version supplied by the author.

linear and went through the democratic figures of public and state institutions. Behind that term stood the idea of a centralized political representation of popular interests: on the one hand there was the freedom of private individuals and the freedom of the markets; on the other, there was the popular solidity of the values of equality and freedom and the guarantee given these values by great public institutions – precisely public – and by the state. But perhaps there is something else behind the difficulties that Arendt indicates, something that *today is no longer unspoken*: by 'the public' she means more than what is legally and institutionally public, namely the fact of being together, of producing together, of building together: in short, what we now no longer call 'the public' but 'the common'. This difference is not simply one of meaning; it also probably has an ontological relevance.

So let us start by asking: has the public really been weakened? And, if it has, how far has this weakening gone? How deep has it gone, this loss of confidence in political representation and in the state's ability to act in the general interest? Above all, has a new sentiment of the common really begun to assert itself through a function of opposition to the public and a new feeling of the common, as if it were a new expression of natural law? And, if it has, to what extent? I feel that this sense of the common is becoming generalized, especially at this moment: this current crisis (economic, social and political) is something of a broomstick from God that cancels out long historical periods and old conceptualizations and lands us in a situation of deep uncertainty and disorientation – but also of great expectation. It is full of doubts, however, and leaves us facing some kind of unknown – the exhaustion of a life experience, of a culture that seems to have reached a limit: and then what will happen? It is within this experience that the concept of the common can help us with discussing and planning an attempt to find an ethical and political way out of the current crisis – as we move with caution.

The public and its institutions are exhausted and freedom cannot be transmitted through the publicness of experience and contemporary life. But why does the sense of the common seem to be expressed in a naïve and powerful way? Now the aspiration to the common seems to arise out of the difficulties of living the crisis. With poverty, it imposes the need to resist, to do things together, to rediscover a 'we' – and this desire is not simply reactive to the critique of the markets' action, which seems increasingly irrational, and of capitalism and big business, which seem to have simply become an experience of enjoying rents. They gamble on completely disembodied financial markets where various phantasmagorias are exercised – of money that produces money, of an unstoppable rent, of a perpetual expansion of speculation – and there is nothing left to remind us of the heroism or, less romantically, the risk of the entrepreneur. Is it in the light of this disaster that the desire for the common is born?

In attempting an answer, I would like to propose four behavioural types for the human being who lives in today's society and suffers the crisis: the 'indebted' person, the 'mediatized' person, the 'securitized' person, and the (politically) 'represented' person.

The *indebted person* is not hard to find. There is a debt situation that arises from the normal conditions under which we live today: in the reality of our working lives we move in a situation of precariousness, which becomes morally heavy and often unsustainable as a way of life. Today there are fewer and fewer situations of production in which one is normally employed, directly productive and normally waged. Rather there are situations of unemployment and precarious employment, always mediated by debt (involving banks, family and friends) and dominated by a totally irrational social distribution of income, in which any reasonable measure of work and consideration for the social value of labour are sidelined. In such conditions, when you work (and also when you are on the dole) it almost feels as if you were in debt to society, and you experience a kind of fragility of your working condition and a liquefaction of the value of your labour. Since the dissolution of big industry and of the Fordist structuring of labour, capitalist value creation has expanded so as to affect the whole of life (and the kind of labour required is one in which the cognitive and social components of production have become increasingly important). Accumulation no longer occurs simply in factories, in the places and at the times of direct labour, but occupies the entire length of a person's lifetime; and capital's occupation of the entire space of life has also transformed all services and all communications into structures of production. The economy has become a bioeconomy, politics has become a biopolitics. It is in this condition that we come to understand what exploitation is today: something that occupies the whole of life but that, in our own lives, expresses itself as precarity and poverty, debt and uncertainty, lack of a future and absence of hope.

As for the *mediatized person*, we are and will continue to be more and more immersed in mediatization, on the one hand because cognitive labour, the work of the brain, the work of communication – in short, immaterial labour – are increasingly the key to productive work, and therefore to accumulation; on the other hand, because in mediatization we not only work but also are held prisoner. We are surrounded by a world of ghosts, by opinions that try to shape us, by messages that artificially condition our emotions, our concepts, and above all our patterns of consumption. Is it possible once again to describe this situation with a word that has rather fallen into disuse – alienation? I believe so, given that, in these communication-saturated spaces that we inhabit, we no longer have a sense of actual truth. What I am arguing against here is not just a naïve perception of reality that can be resolved in the nostalgic re-finding of natural or innate truths; it is rather a desire for a criterion that, in this mediatized horizon where we are prisoners of sorts, could help us to express relationships and affects and to rebuild values. The problem is thus how to find again, in and only in a world that has been radically transformed, real relationships of language, of values, in order to be able to take action.

Then there is the *securitized person*, the person who is ferociously dragged, in every moment of their life, towards a sense of being 'endangered'. 'You are in danger!' This is the warning on which power has always been built: fear and more fear, constructed as a fundamental relationship that is realized in relations between people. From this point of view, human beings, citizens, are introduced into a world of terrifying phantasms that haunt them continually (checks, searches, demands for attention, dangers threatened or whispered, remote control, theft of personal data and so on); the state should free them from these ghosts. In reality it always pushes them back into fear, angst, the nightmare of misery, crime, crisis and – why not? – war. We have only to think of the spectres that haunt the processes of migration, both in the heads of those who migrate and in the heads of those who receive them. This is a world shaken by demons, around which horrible feelings coagulate that then express themselves socially and politically.

The last type is that of the *represented person*, in other words the person who seeks a residual safety, or at least a guarantee of security, in the political sphere, in political representation. The represented person is the person in pursuit of happiness, to use American constitutional terms; and what do they get under today's constitutional conditions? Inefficiency, corruption, falsehood, irresponsibility – in short, all the disgraces that current 'democratic' politics offers us. Behind these experiences there now lies an increasingly intense, massified suffering. There is therefore something that crushes life into money and afflicts it in debt, something that lends an air of hysteria to the domination of the media, to the worry of insecurity and to the failure of decent political representation – in short, something that leaves us in a very unhappy situation.

Yet at this point, from which there is no escape, we have to ask once again: *how can one be free?*

Perhaps it would be worth analysing the four situations that I have described, to ask whether in them, beyond the negativity that characterizes them, there are not powers [*potenze*] that can allow us better to understand the kind of resistance that is necessary, and therefore to approach the question raised at the outset: what is this desire for the common that emerges today in the crisis? Debt and the dominance of financial structures, what are they in fact? They are in the first place a recognition that working life or productive life has never been as cooperative as it is today: we depend on one another in an absolutely profound way. What capital calls debt is in fact our mutual dependence in cooperation. Today production no longer develops through command, but through cooperation. Cognitive labour has become hegemonic in the process of value creation. But what is cognitive labour? It is a putting together of singularities in labour; *certainly this is a model, often fraught with perverse or pathological repercussions* – but it is very true that, when we examine the current organization of labour, we can recognize that there is less and less need for capitalist command to organize them: it is the workers, in their cognitive productivity, who organize their work among them, autonomously. This is a fine trend and it is real and actual; it is as a result of this trend that society has become more productive.

A reflection is required at this point. This is not to say that exploitation has disappeared; neither has it become any less horrible. What has changed is the powers to resist and the hope for liberation. In a productive society in which every use value has become an exchange value, in which the boss's domination reaches into every corner of life, in which it is the financial measure, defined by an anonymous power, that establishes the general relationship with the mass of labour that is captured by society – in such a society the rebellion can become stronger, building on awareness that from now on people produce not only if they are organized by the boss; they can also produce cooperatively, organizing themselves autonomously. At the very moment in which it makes you unhappy, debt also reveals that today's production is done in an eminently cooperative way.

This is how even the fear that holds you subjected can be overcome – through the trust that we have in others and in the forms of life that we organize and in which we take militant action to defend ourselves from the bad things that are heaped upon us. We know that the attacks we suffer, the immiseration that precarity and unemployment impose, are capable of being resisted – because it is we who are the strength of life, its quality, and its productivity. We, too, are the strength of the common we build. Education and the processes of construction of common forms of life and production can give us the guarantee of a society in which people do not have to live in fear of one another.

This lived affirmation of the common goes alongside a transformative activity that requires that private property and its public guarantee be removed and that the common and its use become a fundamental right of citizens. Here enormous constitutional problems arise, because in modern constitutions the common does not exist; there is just the private – and the public that protects it. We therefore have to begin to think that in a constitution of the common the concept of property is no longer something that invests and forms institutions, but something subordinate to the purposes of common use and management of production and wealth. The *common* means overcoming poverty and misery; it is a reaction to the conditions of exploitation and alienation that now condition not only the weakest parts of society but the whole of life – subsumed as it is under the domination of capital. Common means an ability to express wealth through free cooperation. *This is the common!* Today the exercise of a constituent power that renews society and the state and inaugurates the common is the only way in which the problems of freedom can be addressed – the imagining of a new society, founded no longer on a freedom that is subjected to private property but on a freedom that consists in the ability to establish a common relationship between singularity and multitude.

But let us return rather to that being out of joint* – labour in our society. It is the transformation of labour that has put life in crisis and that therefore requires a renewal of the form of work and life. This all started with the 1970s. During the crisis of that decade, the technical composition of labour underwent deep changes. As I have already stated, capital extended the valorization processes to the whole society. In so doing, it pushed forward a slow but continuous transformation of material labour into immaterial labour. It also developed the conditions for cognitive labour to become hegemonic within the processes of production. Second, it brought the biopolitical fabric of society into production. To accomplish this, it developed exploitation by outsourcing work from the factory, by making it precarious, by collecting the benefits of its social diffusion and by

---

* 'out of joint' in English in the original.

capturing its cooperative nature. These two processes – the cognitivization and the socialization of labour – make the great transition that we have definitively witnessed of late. Here what is required by capital as an essential basis for valorization is the very production of workers' subjectivity. I need hardly point out how radically the temporalities, the temporal standards* of labour have been transformed by these changes: if the whole life is put to work, then temporality is no longer a measure but the liquid envelope in which workers produce.

So at this point financialization ends up as the only horizon for capturing and measuring social labour in this new mode of production. Inasmuch as finance (and only it) constructs and imposes the measure of social labour, and inasmuch as it invests life and forms of life and configures them within the measure of money, it is clear that 'profit' and 'wages' are now given in the form of 'rent' or 'debt'. And it is also clear (for those who wish to see) that, by operating in this way, finance invades the sphere of public regulation of society more than ever before in the history of capitalism. The result is a *progressive private patrimonialization* [patrimonializzazione] *of the public*, of the public domain, as well as of the domain of regulation. The welfare state† is privatized and sovereignty is patrimonialized, to such an extent that the life of citizens is put totally into production. This is the point of the ultimate paradox, at which the structures of welfare (school, health, demographic reproduction and so on) and social cooperation (communication, culture, transport and so on) become a terrain for accumulation and for the value creation of capital.

But at this point resistance arises, too. We have already seen this in part. Now let us look at it again, not only in its genealogy but also in the dispositifs that it produces. We know that capital, like any political institution (because capital is a political institution, as Marx established, taking over the concept of power developed by Machiavelli and Spinoza, and as Foucault later reiterated), is a relationship: as a power, it is the outcome of an action on the action of another, of a command that encounters resistance, of the action of fixed capital against the working class and the proletariat. Therefore, if every action produces a reaction and if in socialized capitalism capital presents itself as biopower, then proletarian resist-

---

* 'standards' in English in the original.
† 'welfare state' in English in the original.

ance is biopolitical and, in confrontation, plays upon the irreducible potential of cognitive and cooperative excedence – developing it in forms that are constituent.

This series of statements obviously needs to be developed. Here is not the place to do so (but in the tradition of workerist thought these concepts have already been constructed and demonstrated many times in practice, and the developing researches on the relationship between Marx and Foucault confirm this). However, it should be added that, again from a phenomenological point of view, the potential for resistance exhibits a constant (albeit relative) autonomy.

In fact knowledge is not unilaterally constructed or produced by capital in the cognitive subjects, in the immaterial workers; in most cases they form themselves autonomously, and the more precarious the cognitive workforce is, the more it can (and perhaps knows how to) present itself as 'independent'. We then simply note that the new technical composition of the cognitive proletariat may entail a new political potentiality. It is not certain that this will happen; but if it does, the break that the cognitive workforce determines merely by not being built in rarity, in scarcity, in the necessity of capitalist command (as happened in the factory-society) but by forming itself autonomously – in autonomy, with an excedence of power (as intelligence always is), up to the creation of independent structures – could bring about the definitive splitting of the 'One', of capitalist power. In this case, the drive towards plurality would be given in an irresistible way, in the face of a capitalism, now revealed as biopower, which tends systematically to constitute itself as oneness [*unità*].

It is in this perspective that the movements of 2011 expressed new political modalities in the face of the problems raised by the crisis. I therefore want to develop some further considerations on them, to conclude this phenomenology of living in the crisis. Let's start again from the alienation of the represented person. Represented persons are deprived of the possibility of expressing themselves politically, that is, of expressing their will and knowledge of the social relationship, of directing it towards happiness. Political representation today, or rather representative democracy itself, is an instrument of domination formed and subjected by money, by wealth, by the 1 per cent over the 99 per cent. Political representation has been reduced to capital assets. Rebelling against this representative subjection to the money of the powerful and to the measures of wealth means rediscovering that freedom, equality and solidarity live on a common ground, which is that of life built by the workers, by those who produce and who want, quite simply, to be free and equal.

I don't have an answer to this question. But let us proceed on the basis of the experiences that are beginning to embody, and to give shape and language to, new figures of radical democracy. In the movements that appeared in 2011, we can identify two fundamental characteristics.

The first involves the expression of an autonomous temporality. Anyone who has followed the history of social and political movements in the West since the Second World War, and especially since 1968, will have noticed how often (almost always, in fact) they emerged in the form of a reaction, in other words in response to unforeseen historical events or incidents. Then the development of these movements usually advances in the rhythm of a response to the decisions of power. The motions of power have almost always anticipated those of the democratic movements. The movements of 2011, on the other hand, have shown a marked independence and autonomy in the management of their own development, in the grading of their constituent power. These movements exhibit new characteristics in their definition of temporality, but also in the determination of their own spatial location. This suggests that a dynamic ontology of social being can be proposed here in original and radical forms.

For example, when one examines the long and expansive temporality of the Arab Spring, it might seem that a conception of time is surreptitiously introduced that is different from the insurrectional acceleration of events that normally defines the beginning of any struggle. But this is not the case: the decision process in open, horizontal assemblies, a process that has characterized all the 'camps' of 2011, is also very slow. What is interesting and new in these struggles is not their speed or slowness, but rather the political autonomy with which they manage their own temporality. This marks a huge difference from the rigid or hysterical rhythms of the alter-global movements, which were following the meetings* of government summits at the beginning of this century. On the contrary, in the 2011 cycle of struggles, speed, slowness, deep intensity and superficial accelerations are combined and mixed. At each moment, time is snatched from the programming imposed by external pressures and by the timings of elections, and rather establishes its own calendar and rhythms of development. This notion of *autonomous temporality* helps us to clarify why we see these movements as presenting *alternatives*. In fact an alternative is not an action, a proposal, or a

---

* 'meetings' in English in the original.

discourse simply opposite to the programme of power but rather a new dispositif, rooted in an asymmetrical point of view. This point of view lies elsewhere. Its autonomy renders coherent the rhythms of its own temporality, and in this perspective it produces new subjectivity, struggles and constituent principles.

And here we have the second characteristic of these constituent movements. The temporal determinations of a constituent action fluctuate between latency and rapidity in relation to other factors as well. The most important thing is how contagious, or rather epidemic, each constituent action can be. Asking for freedom in the face of a dictatorial power, for example, introduces and spreads the idea of an equal distribution of wealth – as happened in Tunisia and Egypt; placing the desire for democracy against the traditional structures of political representation also raises the need for participation in transparency, as in Spain; protesting against the inequalities created by financial control also leads to the demand for a democratic organization of the common and for free access to it, as in the United States; and so on. The defence of a park in Istanbul becomes a struggle against the clericalism of thought and power throughout Turkey; the protest against rising transport prices in São Paulo becomes a protest throughout Brazil against the watering down of the Lulist anti-poverty revolution and against the exclusion of a recently emancipated multitude. Temporalities are fast or slow, according to the viral intensity of communicating ideas and desires that, in every case, establish singular syntheses. There is obviously no 'autonomy of the political' in the Schmittian sense here; the constituent decisions of the protest camps are formed through complex constructions and negotiations of knowledge. There is no leader or central committee that decides. Method becomes essential, as does the programmatic discourse: the Spanish *indignados* and the occupiers of Wall Street combine in their discourse and action the critique of representative political forms and a protest against social inequality and domination by finance.

The struggles of 2011 took place in markedly different places, and their protagonists lead very different kinds of lives. Why, then, do we consider these struggles to be part of the same cycle? First, it is obvious that they face the same enemy, characterized by its power in matters of debt: the media, security regimes and a corrupt system of political representation. The first point to emphasize is that practices, strategies and objectives have been able to connect and combine various plural struggles into a singular project, to create a common ground, albeit with differences. The glue that holds it all together can initially be linguistic, cooperative- and network-based, but this common language soon spreads through horizontal decision-making processes.

The process requires temporal autonomy. This often begins with small communities or neighbourhood groups (in Tel Aviv the Israeli *indignados* reproduced the spirit and political form of the kibbutz tradition)... Such movements have tried to find support and inspiration in federalist models. Small groups and communities connect with one another and create common projects without abandoning their differences. Federalism thus constitutes an engine for recomposition. Of course, very few elements of the theory of the state and federalist sovereignty are to be found here; rather there is the residue of the passions and intelligence of a federal logic of association. It is no coincidence, on the other hand, that many of the weapons developed against these movements are animated by the project of breaking the connections of these federalist logics. Religious extremism often serves to divide movements in the Arab countries; vengeful and racist forms of repression have been used to divide insurgents in Britain; and in North America, Spain and elsewhere in Europe police provocations aim to push non-violent protests into violence as a way of creating divisions.

Here, through these movements, politics is conquering a pluralistic ontology. A true pluralism of struggles emerges from different traditions and expresses different objectives, which combine in a federative and cooperative logic to create a model of constituent democracy; in this model differences have the ability to interact and build new institutions – from below but with great effective power, just as Spinoza wanted: against global capital, against the dictatorship of finance, against the biopowers that are destroying the earth, and for free access to and self-management of the common. At the next stage, these movements will not only live new human relationships but also participate from below in the construction of new institutions. While up until now we have built the politics of plurality, from now on we will have to set in motion the ontological machine of plurality itself. A plural ontology of politics has been set in motion, from 2011 until today, through the encounter and recomposition of militant subjectivities.

For me, this is what it means to live the crisis: to discover, within it, a new *conatus* and a new *cupiditas* of happiness.

Part II

The Fundamentals

3

In Search of *Commonwealth*[*]

1. Many problems remained open after *Empire* and *Multitude*. There is no point in restating them here, just as it had been useless to try to close them. Rather it was a question of starting over again, on the basis of the concepts that had been established, in order to go deeper into the question: what is politics today? What is subversive politics, what sharing [*partage*] of the social does it envisage? How can capital be fought today? The unsolved problems can be faced with new strength, but only if we press forward; of this I am convinced. However, at the end of ten years of work on *Empire* and *Multitude* we[†] had a strong sense – a perception by now mature – that our present had redefined itself, that the time when this present could be determined under the prefix 'post-' was over. We had definitely lived through a transition; so, now, what were the symptoms of its end? It seemed to us that the central point on the agenda was the concept of democracy. The concept had been exhausted in the American wars, through the frenzied propaganda made on that front by neoconservatives. Other things, which the concept of democracy could no longer encompass, emerged in the field of political science. I need only refer, by way of illustration, to Rosanvallon and what he tries to grasp and describe in his latest book, *La contre-démocratie: La politique à l'âge de la défiance*: something profound has gone, he tells us – from the republic, from the modern behaviour of populations; and it is now impossible to find it. It is something obscure, which we can no longer

---

[*] First published as Antonio Negri, 'À la recherche du Commonwealth', *Rue Descartes*, 6.17 (2010): 6–17. doi: 10.3917/rdes.067.0006.

[†] Michael Hardt and Antonio Negri, co-authors of *Empire*, *Multitude* and *Commonwealth*.

explain. This is how he tries to account for the feelings of mistrust and powerlessness, the figures of depoliticization that shape contemporary democracy. And he adds – reluctantly, one feels – that 'political democracy' has become a sign behind which a 'mixed regime' has now been consolidated that had to include a *counter-democracy*, a 'democracy of exception'.

This attempt, in political science, to effect a synthesis on such an uncertain reality is repeated in economic science. There the effort is to reinvent, not a *measure* of development (long unavailable after the crisis of the classical law of labour value), but a new effective *convention*, since it is now recognized that the liberal–libertarian convention and the Fordist, Keynesian, or welfare state convention are in crisis. (For example, we often hear of an 'energy convention', but nobody really knows what that means, except that, when it also includes nuclear power, as is often said, it is opposed to the 'ecological convention', and consequently perhaps also to the democratic convention. Al Gore seems to have asked this question.)

Finally, the attempt at reflection in international politics (along with the search for a global political science) involves reinterpreting the global dimension of power multilaterally today, when American unilateralism (that is, what remained of the old imperialism), having been defeated, is in profound crisis. Note how the criticisms that had been levelled at us – of not recognizing the continuity of imperialism in the global action of the American government – are now demystified. In fact, after the crisis of unilateralism, we still remain *within* a global order. Its effects – exhaustion of the nation state, dissolution of international law, multilateral governance* of a single global market – begin to be admitted inasmuch as historical actors are forced to act within this new reality, which previously they hypocritically denied. The recognition of the new order is therefore practical rather than theoretical, but nonetheless effective!

So we have passed through a long period of ambiguity and paradoxes: the postmodern was a culture of transition and represented, in the figures of randomness and uncertainty, alternatives of an unsolvable complexity, internal to this period of transition. Today the transition has been completed. There has been a definitive break, and it is one that has paradoxical consequences. For example, within the perceived aleatory nature of history and the supposed complexity of its systems, the ideologies of the right and the left, far from

---

* 'multilateral governance' in English in the original.

disappearing, have superimposed themselves on one another and are now mixed and confused. *The neutralization of the political* has come about through the most diverse positions' rush towards an extreme centre: a real extremism of the centre appeared in this way. In each experience and place of democracy, an attempt is made to consolidate a *post-ideological* point, a neutral centre, in order to get out of the chaos. Can one perhaps say that, just as the baroque thermidor and the Counter-Reformation invented sovereignty at the end of the Renaissance revolution, between Machiavelli and Bodin, so today we are trying to invent something new, useful and matched to the new exigencies? But what is that something?

To begin to orient ourselves, to try to find a sure way between these uncertainties, these caesuras, and these questions, let us say that we start from *the contemporary*, pure and simple. The crisis has run its course. It is impossible to go back. We have to begin to move within the determinations of the new era, but without ever losing sight of the episode of the transition.

2. What is it that the objective determination of the new historical condition rests on, through and after the crisis of the modern order? What follows is a first attempt at analysis.

From the point of view of state critique, the point is that *the sovereign synthesis is in crisis*. That the crisis is definitive is shown by the process of becoming precarious – or, better, by the deficit in the deductive mechanism of the law, as defined in judicial modernity, in nineteenth-century constitutionalism, and in the theories of the state of right [*stato di diritto*] or rule of law.* Both in their hard continental version and in their Atlantic jurisprudential version, these sovereign practices are no longer able to construct and guarantee *the government of the concrete*. Legitimacy and effectiveness of the law are now at a distance from each other.

The Weberian model that considers sovereignty or legitimacy from a rational–functional point of view has run its course. The hypermodern attempt to restore instrumental logics to the government of the concrete is also incapable of arriving at sensible conclusions. The fact is that the government of the concrete has ceased to be what it was for 'modern' constitutionalism and administrative action. The concrete is not the individual end point of a juridical decision, but a substantial and living network – *biopolitical*, we might say – and acting on it

---

* 'rule of law' in English in the original.

means gathering its activity. At one time the juridical act imposed itself on the real; now the juridical act confronts biopolitical reality, collides with it, and reshapes itself through contact with it.

In the view of the most watchful constitutionalists and administrators, for example the likes of Luhmann and Teubner, and also according to jurists who operate in the more open fields of labour and business law (domestic and international alike), juridical action will no longer have the capacity to be deployed deductively; it will rather consist, on each occasion, in the solution of a singular conflict – a solution whose form traditional dogmatics does not foresee – and therefore in the determination of a provisional mediation, of a transitory dispositif. The concrete is split, no government activity can be given in a linear way any more. Only governance* is given. Warning: when we speak of governance, we move in a minefield. Governance is not in itself a democratic tool; it is rather a managerial dispositif. What opens this machine to democracy is use matched to democratic interests, and thus a democratic exercise of force that effectively opposes another exercise of force (possibly oriented non-democratically). The importance of this instrument and its possible democratic opening derive not from 'nature', but from the sociopolitical consistency of the actors. At this point, the constitutionalists sometimes go as far as to introduce the concept of a constitutionalism without a state, in other words the practice of a permanent and continuous redefinition of subjective right, of the rights of the parties, and in general of the conventions of agreement. But, if one is less optimistic, it is now necessary to recognize that the old conception of law and the new biopolitical consistency of reality are at odds. Every solution leads back to *biopower* – but this is without measure, and is therefore capable only of exception; and then the biopolitical instances arise and propose alternatives to great effect.

The one has divided into two: here is a good first paradigm of contemporaneity. To say this is not to say 'no' to the multiple. The paradigm implies only an ability (and perhaps strength) to question whether *another horizon* might now be forming through every terrain of jurisprudential plurality and constitutional articulations: a horizon in which new constituent powers [*poteri costituenti*] are expressed, and hence a terrain on which the classic definition of *constituent power as an original, extra-juridical power* is abandoned in favour of a juridical conception of constituent power as a *potenza* internal to the legal

---

* 'governance' in English in the original.

system and indefinitely whole. This is a central point in our book *Commonwealth*, when it comes to defining political contemporaneity. We will see later how the very concept of revolution has to bend to this renewal of constituent power and thus to its definition as an 'internal source of right', and therefore also to the possibility that the revolution acts within the constitutions, in other words within constituted power, in an untiring way. On the other hand, here one can say that temporality comes to be reinserted centrally into the definition of right.

3. Now we need to deepen the objective determination of the new contemporary condition, opening – so to speak – its second movement. So far we have followed the transition from a political–institutional point of view: crisis of sovereignty, governance, redefinition of constituent power. Now we have to raise the problem from the point of view of labour, of its organization, of the power relations that traverse it.

Who is it that produces? In today's world, it is the machine of the multitude. Production is social. The hegemonic form of productive labour is cognitive labour. We have definitively arrived at a new sequence: living labour, cognitive labour, cooperative production (i.e. social cooperation), biopolitical fabric of production, and so on and so forth. The relationship between the technical composition (TC) and the political composition (PC) of labour power has been extraordinarily transformed and complicated. At one time the TC represented the potential – often only virtual, sometimes real – of a matching PC. Now, in today's world, in the regime of cognitive labour, virtuality and potentiality are mutually implicated in the relationship and constitute its nature and dynamics. Rather than corresponding to each other and creating isomorphisms, TC and PC hybridize, crossbreed. There was a certain dialectic, for example in the workers' narratives of the historical relationship between class (on the side of TC) and party (on the side of PC) that took place during the class struggle, with its periodical ups and downs and especially its cyclical dimensions. Now, in the current biopolitical condition, this dialectic no longer exists – or exists much less. The biopolitical fabric confuses the relationship between TC and PC, but at the same time extends it and breaks that dependence on the industrial organization, over which direct capitalist command was still exercised with great effectiveness.

Bearing these observations in mind, we are able to grasp the moment of crisis: in the great transformation under way, command *leaves out the new figure of living labour.* Living labour has become singularized in the biopolitical and is now socialized *independently* of the capitalist organization of labour. This brings us to a second paradigm of contemporaneity.

At the very moment when capital, qua biopower, subsumes society entirely, the process of integrating labour power into capital is fully revealed and the disjunction between labour power and capital is radicalized. Workers express their biopolitical and productive capacity within the entire circuit of social production. Here the bodies become socially active and the soul materializes in productive labour; consequently, it is the whole that gives meaning to the singular labour contribution, just as, by way of comparison, it is the singular linguistic contribution that gives meaning to a linguistic whole. Capital and labour power are played out entirely in *bios* ('life'), but precisely here capital and labour are also separated, as a system of biopowers against the *biopolitical fabric or power*.

Consequently the worker is no longer faced with capital, except in the most indirect and abstract form of *rent*, in other words as capital that multiplies the more general, territorial expropriation, or in the financial figure, that is, as expropriator of the whole social valorization of labour, monetarily expressed. If you look at it from this angle, given the relative interdependence of cognitive and socially cooperative labour, it is not just profit that workers are faced with, but profit transformed into rent: they are no longer faced with the individual capitalist as the organizer of exploitation but with the *collective capitalist* as financial mystifier of social labour.

Just as Marx had spoken of a 'socialism of capital' in connection with the birth of joint stock companies, today we can metaphorically propose a kind of communism of capital, in which capitalism produces the absolute mystification of a valorization that, given what was said earlier, is immediately common and exploits directly the social participation in valorization – that is, the *sociality* of the worker.

We can add a further question: does this happen in a parasitic way? Perhaps. It is certain that, if capital exploits and mystifies the common wealth, it ceases organizing its production process. Capital continues to present itself as power and, since production is immersed in life, as biopower. Exploitation therefore passes today through the social organization of biopowers. Whether this organization is parasitic or not makes little difference.

But to this reflection on the autonomy of the *productive subject* we must add – and this is what we do in *Commonwealth* – other reflections, on the autonomy of the *resistant subject*. I want briefly to introduce here another argument that has been developed in part, but not sufficiently: its relative absence from our past work has been rightly accounted as negative, and even deplored as a substantial limitation of our research. I don't think that this is how things are. In fact I would like to point out that, in order to add to our work (*Empire* and *Multitude*) the 'missing chapter' on the coloniality of power (for this is, obviously, what was meant), it would have been necessary first of all to excavate and rediscover the truth about a *non-identitarian* solidity and movement of anti-colonial struggles and of the subjects who were active in them. It was therefore necessary to pass not only through the theories of postcoloniality but through the emancipatory and liberating practices of colonized peoples and of movements of political liberation in the *non-regressive* continuity of their development. A revisiting of Frantz Fanon's lesson was essential for us in this regard. But not only that: the contribution to this process made by the Zapatista movement was fundamental precisely because it avoided any insistence on identity, removed any misunderstanding about national–popular alternatives, illustrated the ambiguity, sometimes simply reactionary, of certain indigenist theories, and insisted on the constituent potentialities that came from the accumulation of resistance. To repeat myself, it was certainly possible, if not easy, to address that revision, which we had to make, from a historiographical point of view; on the other hand, it would have been impossible to give it the intensity of a theoretical reading, of a political proposal, as long as the anti-colonial resistance movements and the democratic consistency of the liberation processes developed by them had not displayed the characteristics of contemporaneousness. Theory follows the real. It is therefore not identity but constituent resistance that testifies to the success of the march of freedom. To find legitimacy, postcolonial theories have to move beyond the hermeneutics of past struggles and indicate, well beyond the archaeology, the genealogy and course of the present revolution. This is what is happening, and it is what every revolutionary theory of transformation in the contemporary world has to assume as a method. With this, once again, the ontological autonomy of the multitude, the continuity and accumulation of the production of subjectivity, and the irreducible antagonism of biopolitical power against biopower – in this case, colonial biopower – come to be documented. That subject, which managed to resist the coloniality of power through a very singular experience of exodus (continuous distancing from the colonizer, possible tactics and episodes of hybridization, pressing insurrections, etc.) – well, that subject reveals itself more and more to be a constituent force.

This completes the objective topography that, in *Commonwealth*, displays the insuperable obstacles to the stabilization of capitalist power in the contemporary world.

NB. From a philosophical point of view, in paragraphs 2 and 3 we share the experience – in our contemporary times, in the face of living cognitive labour and postcolonial resistance – and we elaborate on the impossibility for capital to conclude the process of exploitation, that is, the very realization of capitalist domination. In this respect, the end of the dialectic is no longer an abstract instance but a phenomenological determination. It follows that, with the irreversibility of this transition, the new horizon of subjectivity is fixed in the present: singularity is contingency, difference, autonomy, resistance – and therefore constituent power.

4. Let us now deal with the subjective dispositifs of the new political condition in the contemporary world. Here is a first movement.

Activity on the biopolitical terrain reveals itself in the form of a *production of subjectivity*. But what does 'production of subjectivity' mean? Given the conditions defined so far, the production of subjectivity is an expression of forms of life and, through these, a process of production and valorization of the common. We have in fact seen that the production of forms of life today has to take place, inevitably, in the dimension of the common. Only the common, in fact, is the form and content of constituent action. Nothing would be constituted unless the common gives meaning to the singularities and the singularities give meaning to the common. But if this is what the production of subjectivity is – namely an enhancement of the common of life, of the totality of all forms of life (which passes through education, health, social peace, security of wages and reproduction, urbanism and everything else) – then the production of subjectivity also opens up a terrain of contestation of biopowers, of capital's attempt to subsume and exploit the common products of life. Thus the antagonism between biopower and biopolitical powers starts here; and then the production of subjectivity is tendentially defined as *exodus from capital*. It is a biopolitical action that exits from the articulations of biopowers.

Can we then define exodus as a process of reappropriation of the common?

Let me set a Spinozan machine in motion. As we know, for Spinoza the production of subjectivity (or the unfolding of the process that leads from sensible *conatus* to rational *amor*) tends to appear as a production of the social. But there is something more, in Spinoza's judgement: a transformation of the social into the common. This means that the production of subjectivity, which integrates and enriches the cooperative production of the social, can become production of the common, when it imposes on itself a radical democratic management of society.

Faced with this Spinozan appropriation of the common (which, in modernity, constitutes an internal and powerful alternative), it is necessary to recall here how the hegemonic categories of private and public came to be formed in modernity. These categories were built on the concept of labour. In fact Locke's definition of the private is a definition of the singular appropriation of the labour performed by the individual. The private is what is one's own, consolidated in juridical form; it is private property.

As for the concept of the public, in the culture of modernity it, too, moves within these same parameters. It is a paradox, but one no less effective: the public alienates 'its own' in order to safeguard its consistency. Therefore the concept of what is one's own is still at the basis of the concept of what is public. The mystification of modernity rests on an almost permanent repositioning of two terms that correspond to two ways of appropriating the common of human beings. One is the use of the category 'private'; the other is the use of the category 'public'. Concerning the former, property – represented, as Rousseau said, by the first man who said 'this belongs to me' [*ceci est à moi*] – is an appropriation of the common by an individual, which means an expropriation of all others. Today private property consists in the denial of the common right of humans to that which only their cooperation can produce. But our good Rousseau, who is so harsh on private property as to make it the source of all corruption and human suffering, loses his head when it comes to the other category – the public. Here is the problem of the social contract – the problem of modern democracies: since private property generates inequalities, how can one invent a political system in which everything, while belonging to everyone, does not belong to anyone? '*Does not belong to anyone*': that's where the public is. It is that which belongs to everyone and to nobody – in other words that which belongs to the state. But the state is not what we produce in common, what we invent and organize as a common. The state refers us to our identity and our nature, gathering from it the concept of common. But then, given that the common no longer belongs to us (since *to be* is not *to have*), the state's getting its hands on the common under the name of public management, delegation or public representation is in reality the creation and justification of another form of alienation.

In short, what is public is still based on what is one's own, making it general; the public bases itself on the 'one' – the unit – as an organic assembly of individuals. The public is the identity of the private, and thus of liberal ideology in the most traditional and profound sense.

It is against the private – and therefore against its public subsumption – that the *concept of the common* is raised as a dispositif of radical democratic management of everything that constitutes the fabric of social activity: reciprocity among individuals, the cooperation of singularities, the freedoms of producers. The common is the negation of one's own through the recognition that only this cooperation constitutes the social and that only the common management of it guarantees its continuous renewal.

It is clear that no place remains for traditional political reformism, which contains an idea of progressive reappropriation of wealth by individuals or groups and, consequently, a continuous mediation in relations of capital; none of this is appropriate any more. We are now immersed in a new condition. A new method is established on this terrain: that of the 'march of freedom'. This march is based on and is articulated by biopolitical dispositifs for the construction of the common: it is a risky but ontologically determined project. There is no guarantee that this process can develop, apart from the continuous, pressing, and militant and constituent undertaking that the subjectivities – the multitude of singularities – put to work. The very definition of being a multitude – and, implicitly, of making multitude – confronts here the difficulties – but also, obviously, the power – of constructing or producing the common.

Here a further problem opens up, namely understanding how, to varying degrees, the independence of living labour is articulated with the dependence that in reality it continues to suffer in the transition phase. But have we not already been through that phase? We have, of course – but not through it as a revolutionary transition that sees the constituent power of living labour and its exodus measured in a work of ontological metamorphosis. Hence continuities and discontinuities must always be defined. Basically, when we talked about the hybridization of the technical composition and political composition of today's proletariat and of the impossibility of capturing them in a linear concatenation or in isomorphic correspondences, we were already alluding to these processes of metamorphosis. But here I need to be more precise and emphasize that, from the point of view of political action, this step is crucial. Exodus is not only a process of distancing but also one of *passing through*, and distancing is often built into passing through. Exodus is always transitive, or rather transitional; and the more it is so, the more constituent it is. All this needs to be placed on the foundation of what I have described so far: the *ontological irreversibility* of the multitudinous paths of living labour in the contemporary world and in the process of building the common.

I might add, in the hope of expanding on this topic on another occasion, that the concept of narrative – of grand narrative – is proposed here as an ethical requirement, as a discursive design, and as a wish for a new schematism that is (not transcendental, but) effective – and I mean capable of matching the definition of contemporaneity and the urgencies of constituent practice. How heavy and atrocious was the postmodern claim to get rid of every historical and ideal narrative! It was perhaps useful – an act of methodological scepticism or, better, of libertine abstention – at the moment of defeat of the hope for transformation, at the end of the short century... Useful, in that it allowed an instant of reflection. But it was also an operation designed to spread poison endemically and to produce impotence. Today, again, we have the possibility of rebuilding broad horizons of freedom (it is interesting to note how, already in German historicism, Dilthey had counterposed to relativism the production of subjectivity as much as he had developed a relativist polemic against the eidetic Husserl).

With this we fix the third paradigm of contemporaneity: that of exodus.

5. And so we come to the question of the legitimation and use of force.

The new method, the one based on biopolitical dispositifs for the production of subjectivity and thus for the construction of the common – the Spinozan method that, starting from misery and poverty, builds the social with the ontological power of solidarity, common work and love – well, this method requires strength. It does because the resistances that oppose the process of civil constitution – this expression of the new constituent institutions – are strong too. One must always construct a political diagonal and endow it with force, when one traverses the biopolitical diagram – that is, when the march of freedom opposes from the inside the arrogant presumption of the biopowers.

It is necessary to recall here the theme of theodicy and reflect for a moment on the question of evil. In our *Commonwealth* we devote a long note to this question, arguing against any substantial, negative or ontological conception of evil. We insist more on a privative concept: the bad is that which is opposed to the realization of the good. Thus force is necessary to overcome evil and constitutes it as an essential element in solving the dilemmas of theodicy.

Here again, a paradox needs to be explored: the constituent dispositif contains force. So the line that leads from constituent power to constituted power, from poverty to social wealth, through living labour – that line, built as it is on the recognition of the other and of the common forms of life through solidarity and love or, in a situation of struggle, on the recognition of the other through anger and the exercise of force against every obstacle… well, that line orients the constituent powers towards the common; and these powers are always in transformation. Thus *force builds institution*.

Is it possible to describe the genealogical dynamics of the institution from the bottom up, that is, from the action of the individual and from the common competence of the singularity? I think it is, provided that we define this process as a progressive work of common construction that, having started from processes of collective learning that are so important for self-formation today, manages to build continuously, without fear of possible crises, a normative power fully consistent with the social movements. We are not dealing here just with any institution, then; it is an autonomous institution – it succeeds in creating an organizing space for the movements and proposes lasting normative directions.

As we have just seen with the transition from the public to the common, the institution that produces norms and exercises command must be more than legitimized by the continuous opening of the constituent power; it must be continually renewed through the effective and efficacious participation of the subjects. Money and weapons, said Machiavelli, are the forces that defend the republic. I think it's not a bad idea for us to be on that same line. Money is the productivity of the common; and when *res publica* is replaced by *res communis*, the doing of the multitude becomes common doing. No money is left that is not common – and *res publica*, too, must be critiqued in this respect, as a mystification of capitalist command. This is why, in *Commonwealth*, we developed a long argument against the republic, revisiting how it was born in seventeenth-century England and showing that it was a case of wealth against poverty and the people against the multitude.

And the weapons, then, what are they? For Machiavelli, they are the people's weapons, designed to defend society internally, to ensure the continuous development of the constituent power (of constituent powers) within and beyond the constituted power and to organize defence against all enemies.

So then: this is the fourth paradigm of contemporaneity. After the 'one' divided into two, which is a critique of sovereignty, after the autonomy of living labour, which is the definition of the terrain of biopolitics on which to lay the debate, and after exodus as reappropriation of the common, which attempts to envisage the teleology of the common – now 'weapons for the multitude'.

Weapons for the people serve essentially to eliminate war. This is one of the latest paradoxes to which contemporaneity introduces us. Against war: if the forms of asymmetrical warfare are studied exactly in the way in which the constitution of the common – as against the public – is studied, one understands the subversive significance of the call for weapons for the multitude, as a revelation of the radical conjoining of force and love. No more war. A recognition that asymmetric warfare is a winning weapon. Asymmetric warfare is armed democracy. Enough of war, as well as enough of sovereignty: they were a monstrous pair of twins.

NB: From a philosophical point of view, in paragraphs 4 and 5 I have tried to follow conceptually the dispositifs of the constitution of the multitude in its self-making: I have pursued that potential for construction of the common, organization of force, and lawmaking that the multitude moulds progressively, maybe discontinuously but according to the powers and tendencies of a *materialist teleology*, from below and from within. Here the constituent power of the multitude presents itself as a dispositif of subjectivation ever more internal to the forms of life, and capable of making changes.

6. Can we speak of a *multitudinous class struggle*? If we do, this is only in the terms already defined by the new transition – in other words in affirmative, positive terms, in recognition of a new ontological power that builds new forms of life – new organizations, new institutions – and in this sense recomposes the dimension of politics. At this point it is worth remembering how and to what extent the metropolitan territory is necessary for the production of subjectivity. Why the metropolis? Because the metropolis is encounter and antagonism, producing versus being produced; it actually overturns the act of producing against the fact of being produced, and does so in a space that represents, for the multitude, what the factory represented for the working class.

It is evident that we shall have to remain on this ground, press forward and deepen our research for a long time to come. The metropolitan organization is still far from being able to assert itself, yet it is there that the time of multitudes is spatialized and concretely determined. Within this temporality, completely tied to the necessity of capitalist exploitation, labour power (living labour) will be able to develop resistance and constituent power.

Poverty and love are built in the metropolis: it is in the tension of poverty that the subjectivity of the multitudinous class struggle is being built. Poverty is not simply misery, it is rather the power of living labour that has not yet found its realization. From this point of view, the precariat constitutes the highest representation of those 'birds of the forest' people whom Marx recognized when he studied the case of proletarians expelled through enclosures.* As for love, it is the ontological engine that leads from solitude to community, from poverty to wealth, from subjection to freedom. It is by being put through these tensions that the multitudinous class struggle can be rebuilt – in the metropolis, where precisely the relationship within the proletariat finds the key to its revolutionary project in the necessity of being in solidarity.

7. Back to basics! I have already referred to the opportuneness of returning to the grand narratives of the future: when we go beyond the postmodern, the elements of resistance must be reassembled in a design that hope extends towards a future temporality. What does it mean to go back to basics? It means discerning in the past, in the long history of modernity, the particular line of thought that has turned into an action of transformation. We know the two lines of modernity that developed after the Renaissance: on the one hand the line of immanence, on the other the authoritarian reproposal of the transcendent. For us, the dividing line passes, radically, between these two lines, and the choice inclines towards the line Machiavelli–Spinoza–Marx. This is the genesis and development of the enlightenment [*Aufklärung*] of the multitude.

And yet, in an attempt to recompose modernity in the broadest way and to propose bridges towards it, we re-offered a reading of Kant – again, in *Commonwealth*. Not a new 'return' to Kant but a reading, in other words a discriminant that passes through his thinking.

Two terrains of research can be found in Kant. On the one hand

---

* 'enclosures' in English in the original.

there is a critical, transcendental line. On this terrain, two tensions that precede it clash intensely and confront each other over the interpretation of the nature of the *Aufklärung*. First of all, Habermas reduces the transcendental to a fabric of communication; then Foucault, in his project of constituting the future, assumes that *Aufklärung* is an indication to be bold, to put in place dispositifs that press forward and into action. But in Kant the critique opens to the schematism of reason, in other words to an ontological projection of knowledge and desire. On this terrain, too, there are two tensions that live and run through these dimensions of critique. On one side there is Heidegger, who leads Kantian schematism towards the annihilation of being, towards inoperability, towards *Gelassenheit* as an atopic and neutralizing conclusion of all desire for transformation; on the other side, Kantian schematism produces the 'community of ends', which is an ethical industriousness. It seems to me that here Foucault intersects with Lucien Goldman and Andre Gorz... but also with many others: all those who rethink and renew the ethical project of a 'strong' Spinozism.

4
The Common as a Mode of Production*

People are beginning to speak of 'the common' as a noun. Until recently (and still exclusively in jurisprudence and law) it was spoken of only in a formal way, as something outside any possible ontological definition – something that only the mode of appropriation, private or public, certified and therefore made to exist. Thus we are coming out of a long history (is it coterminous with the era of modernity?), and now the common appears to us as a *reality* – or, better, as *production*. In what follows I shall resume discussion on this definition. For the moment, I return to our theme: the private appropriation of the collective and the common.[1]

In the era of neoliberalism, the private appropriation of the common is manifest in two particularly noticeable forms: the appropriation, by private individuals, of what is *public* (state property, public goods and public services, etc.); and, second, the appropriation of what we call *nature* – the goods of the earth and of the environment, the physical powers [*potenze*] of life and so on. That those assets can be transferred to private individuals seems obvious and does indeed happen. They are material and natural goods, and the fact that they are appropriated does not seem to concern their substance. But these appropriations need to be qualified more carefully. In the first place, because both public and natural goods are inseparable from the historical conditions and the forms of life that shape them and by which they are shaped. There is here a 'common' determination, histori-

---

* First published as 'Il comune come modo di produzione', *Sudcomune*, 1–2 (2017): 22–8. *Sudcomune* is an Italian journal published by DeriveApprodi in Rome.

cally consistent, which could not be removed. But a qualification of this 'common' emerges that is at once formal (because purely extrinsic) and vulgar (because absolutely generic) and that adapts to these acts of appropriation. The discourse becomes more meaningful in the latter instance. I mean that, even if, during the evolution of modernity, natural and public goods have become *commodities* and, in this condition, present themselves immediately as products of capital – that is, precisely as commodities – this reduction constitutes a problem (and often produces repugnance). In fact, although those goods, collective or natural, constitute the very matter of the productive process in the age of mature capitalism, insofar as they are natural, they seem to us nevertheless to belong to a sphere that should be kept intact and free from claims of possession and, insofar as they are public, they seem to us to be for the most part a historical residue of will and collective struggles – and hence they, too, are illegitimately appropriated by private individuals.

They 'seem to us'... Yet we must give in to the evidence and recognize that on this subject habit has appeased the anger and the industrial advantages have cancelled out the moral reservations. Those goods constitute the privileged object of capitalist appropriation – the objective of the private or public juridical dispositif that realizes 'property rights'. It is a juridically legitimate appropriation, which does not differ from, but rather integrates, capitalist appropriation in general – as an appropriation of the value of labour, as an extraction of value and as a legal and political hypostasis of collective production in the form of private and public property. This domination over individual and collective activities that have established public or natural goods as attractive and usable in the construction of forms of life is the very characteristic of capitalist production. And the domination is accentuated, in mature capitalism, by the ever-increasing overlap between the mode of production and forms of life.

True, for some goods (public or natural), there has been talk of a 'common' type of appropriation of ownership in the case of some goods (public or natural) – and for some decades now. Much rhetoric has been expended in this regard; the proposal has been to define a 'third kind' of ownership, a new form of appropriation, beyond those practised today. Yet these definitions have no solidity, because they are based illusorily on an expansive conception of property rights during the period of capitalist maturity: the common is here conceived of either as a functional extension of private property or as a participatory and democratic institution of the public capacity for appropriation. Our proposal is rather to consider the common not as a *third kind* of property but as a *mode of production*. In the light of the 'vulgar' definition mentioned earlier, this seems to be a proper, scientific definition of the common.

Before addressing the theme of the common as a mode of production, let us try to deepen the substantive definition of the common. Now, it seems to me that the common constitutes an ontological base, produced by the human activity of work in the course of history; a bedrock [*soubassement*], an ontological background of social reality, produced by work. What exactly does this mean? It means that the common is always a 'production'; it is nature regulated or transformed, or simply produced. *The common is therefore a resource only insofar as it is a product* – a product of human labour, and therefore in the capitalist regime immediately traversed by power relations.

In the age of cognitive labour, the common subsumes and highlights the qualities of cognitive labour. And, to avoid misunderstandings, let me repeat that, when I speak of 'cognitive labour', I always speak of labour or work, and thus of an expenditure of physical and mental energy – at any rate, of labour that takes place in the continuity of the capitalist relationship and in the asymmetrical form of this relationship: a *discontinuous* continuity, which means a continuity forced into a cyclical rhythm by the movements and struggles that are always open in capitalism, between command over labour and the resistance of labour power. This relationship is asymmetrical because the capital relation is always unequal and irreducible to identity. It is by virtue of this asymmetry that capital is productive – there is an asymmetry in the forces that confront one another in that relationship of capital; and productivity is the result of a complicated intersection and conflict between the power of 'living labour' and the accumulation of 'dead labour'. In the age of general intellect,[*] which presupposes the hegemony of cognitive labour in capitalist production, the new social organization of work is conditioned by an ever greater productive efficacy of cognitive labour, and therefore by an *ontological* pre-eminence of living labour over dead labour in the relation of capital. Now, in this relation, cognitive labour expresses an *organizational initiative of cooperation* and an *autonomous management of knowledge* by comparison with what happened in the industrial age. This means that work has singularized itself and that labour power produces according to its own subjectivation. Nowadays labour power does not manifest

---

[*] Here and passim, 'General Intellect' in English in the original.

The Common as a Mode of Production

itself, in the capitalist relationship of production, just as variable capital. It appears to you as subjectivity, as a singular power. The capital relation, then, will not be crossed by a material, objective contradiction, but also by (in fact primarily by) a subjective antagonism. An autonomous action – strongly subjectivated – is therefore immanent in the capital relation and qualifies its productivity. (Gramsci had already intuited this when, studying the capitalist crisis of the 1920s, he pointed to political movements and to the material resistance of the working class as the antagonist engine of the transformations in production. He concluded that the 'passive revolution' – which accompanied the birth of Fordism – implicitly contained the construction of the individual worker's 'hegemony' over production.) It is on these premises that it will be possible to proceed to the construction of the concept of the common as a mode of production. The 'common' character of production is rendered substantive by a bedrock [*soubassement*] that is not just historical but active, subjective, cooperative, founded on and preconditioned by a cooperative and communal organization of work. So here we are at the beginning of a path of substantive definition of the common in the age of cognitive labour.

This path is difficult, as is always the fate of those who move forward in an era of transition. We are immersed in a process of transformation that takes us from the industrial age (Fordism) to the post-industrial age (the age of general intellect). We are living in a transitory phase, being forced once again into a kind of passive revolution in which the cognitive workforce builds its own space of production and shows its ability to prefigure and prepare the modalities of production. We can recognize this transition as a moment in a trend in which production exhibits forms that can increasingly be described as *biopolitical* – and thus as a moment

(a) when 'political' designates a life that is indistinguishable from productive activity, in the entirety of time and space of a given society. This condition transforms and reconfigures the structure of the working day, making *work* and *life* overlap;
(b) when *bios* designates a tendential totalization of production across the earth's surface. The world of production thus becomes *ecological* in an etymological sense: production subsumes not only *bios* but also *nature*.

Many other specific conditions are being defined within this trend. It follows, for example, that the law of value is in crisis as a law of exploitation based on the temporal measurement of labour values and their abstraction. That law imposed

(a) a measure of temporality (within a homogeneous working day) with which the time of 'necessary labour' and that of 'surplus labour' could be separated;
(b) a closed spatial condition or a concentration of labour, a massified cooperation such as was guaranteed by the scientific organization of work in the factory;
(c) a narrow view on the relationship between productive and unproductive labour. For example, female work, whether domestic or care work, was not normally taken into account in the quantification of value, in the very definition of 'labour power';
(d) a naïve ecological condition or the approach to nature as an independent reality, not yet crossed by capitalist valorization and valorized by productive labour.

So this is the foundation on which the classical theme of the *abstraction* of value was built – or, better, of values fixed in time, spatially determined, qualitatively discriminating and ecologically limited. The capitalist appropriation of the global value of social production – for which we can repeat the epithet of 'vulgar common' – was thus determined through the exploitation of labour and through the abstraction, mediation and equalization of values on this scale. On the other hand, the common – now, in the age of cognitive and cooperative work, of general intellect – has a biopolitical figure and is structured by the production of subjectivity. It is 'common' in the proper, scientific sense. It follows that capitalist appropriation presents a completely transformed figure and the appropriation of surplus labour is no longer exercised through the direct exploitation of labour and its consequent *abstraction*, but rather through a new mechanism of appropriation, characterized by the *extraction of the common* as the constitution of the overall social production. And if this common covers every time and every social space of valorization, if there is no more space outside capitalist production, and if every labour function is subservient to valorization, this extractive exploitation is preconstituted by the autonomous organization of cooperation done by cognitive subjectivities – an independent power within a ferocious machine of exploitation. To put it another way: in the capital relation with its asymmetry, this 'capitalist common' is subjected to an ever more antagonistic tension. Every life has become productive; the extraction of value is performed across the global biopolitical sphere and is not limited to spaces and times explicitly devoted to work.

This overall picture is made possible by the fact that the nature of labour power has changed. Without wishing to reconstruct the entire history of capitalist development in the last century, we can recall how the working-class struggles in capitalist metropolises put the industrial mode of production into crisis in the first half of the twentieth century and how automated production and the socialization of information technology, by investing the society as a whole, determined the progressive consolidation of general intellect in the second half. The massification of labour in factories has been replaced by the singularization of work performance; factory command has been replaced by the cooperative organization of social labour; and the physical effort of manual labour has been replaced by the intellectual undertaking of cognitive activity – in a word, the mass has been replaced by the *multitude*. If the new mode of production arises in these conditions, it can be assumed (as I have repeatedly anticipated) that the common comes *before the capitalist labour market* and before the capitalist social organization of labour – the so-called social division of labour. If the new mode of production, like all capital's modes of production, is a terrain of struggle, in this space the position of cognitive labour is relatively privileged today by comparison with the past, in that it holds *power* [potere] over cooperation, over the organization of work and over the organization of productive knowledge. It follows that capital has to adapt to the common. It suffers its mode of production, changing the characteristics of exploitation and passing from the *abstraction* of industrial values to the *extraction* of the social value of production. However, it loses its entire capacity of command within this new relationship.

And yet, when one studies the theories of *value creation* [valorizzazione] through *extraction*, one cannot fail to notice that this is not something entirely new. In particular, in the chapters of *Capital* on primitive accumulation, Marx gave a broad description of the forms in which common lands and common rights had been obliterated and lands and rights appropriated by nascent capitalism. Without this privatistic appropriation of the common, as Marx correctly observed, the initial accumulation of capital that allowed the start of the manufacturing era, the basis of an industrial society, would not have been possible. But it is clear that there can be no analogy between that pre-capitalist common, whose expropriation is necessary for the construction of capitalism, and the common as it appears in our experience today.

A second formulation of the theory of valorization, by means of extraction (which often reflects Marx's primitive accumulation), can be found in 'western Marxism', from the Frankfurt school to workerism [*operaismo*] and postcolonialism, when labour and production are considered in the light of real subsumption in capital. The passage from formal subsumption to real subsumption is represented by a cycle of subjection and progressive appropriation, by the capitalist, of the labour processes and of productive society itself, in its entirety. In a first, formal phase, capital absorbs spaces and temporalities that have differences; in the second, real phase, capital imposes a homogeneous regime of production, consumption and so on. It can be said that in this case we are passing from the regime of profit to a regime of rent. But this is a rent that has been profoundly modified from its definition in the classics. What is this modification? It is the fact that this rent is extracted directly from a *productive* common. The capitalist appropriation of the common in the real subsumption of society in capital can be recognized as a producer of *rent* only when we assume (and verify) that this appropriation acts on a society prefigured and preconstituted by a substantive activity that produces the common. Hence, even in this case, there is no analogy with the (traditional) definitions of both absolute and relative rent.

How did this new framework come about? The transformation took place essentially in two figures:

(a) One happened when the mode of production became entirely biopolitical. The capitalist command over production penetrated life in its entirety. We have already discussed this. That is, we are witnessing a totalization of exploitation, structured around cognitive labour and its ability to implement cooperation autonomously. It is from this antagonistic condition that the web of life forms is captured by capital. Languages, codes, needs and consumptions, the structure of knowledge and that of desire, in the richness of their singularization, are made available for the extraction processes of capital.

(b) The second figure in which this new form of exploitation is embodied is *financialization*. This represents the form in which capital *measures* the extraction of the common. The measure is expressed by command in its monetary function, that is, by money [*denaro*]. It could be said here that *money is the perverse figure of the common* and its total mystification. In fact we live immersed in money: this is the same as experiencing that we live as subjected beings in the vulgar common, as prisoners of that common productive structure that cognitive labour has created and continues to produce, and that money measures and commands. From this perspective it is clear that the processes of the world of finance are not parasitic but immanent in the organization of valorization.

By way of conclusion, I will say that capital develops the right of *private appropriation* and its public mediation, in the construction of a *financial command* for the *exploitation of the common* (but we will have to talk about this on another occasion).

Once the capitalist appropriation of the common has been described in this way, we have to return and consider the transformations that have taken place in labour power and in technologies, and also those of capital that invests in life and is invested by it. As I have already said, the line of development of capitalist exploitation is *discontinuous* and the capital relation is *asymmetrical*. When we take *the common as a mode of production*, we are describing the result of a transition from the industrial phase to the cognitive phase of productive labour. It goes without saying that this transition is neither linear nor homogeneous. Rather it reproduces discontinuities and asymmetries in bringing its own path to an extreme limit and in representing it in the extraction of the common. Capital here loses its dignity, which consisted in organizing production and in imprinting development on society. Here capital is also forced to reorganize itself and to show its antagonistic nature in an extreme form. This means that *the class struggle develops around the common*. And, from what I have said so far, it appears clearly that there are *two figures of the common*: one is that of a *common* subjected to the capitalist *extraction* of value, the other is that of a *common as an expression* of the cognitive and productive capacities of the multitude. Between these two forms of the common there is not only objective contradiction but also subjective antagonism.

I have already pointed out the steps that made the mode of production turn from an industrial figure to a post-industrial figure, from 'big industry' to 'socialized industry' in the course of the twentieth century. I have also pointed out that these passages contain the transformation of labour power from labour power of the mass worker through labour power of the social worker to labour power of cognitive labour. It would now be worth pointing out that 'cognitive labour' does not refer only to intellectualization of work and deepening of expanded cooperation in production, but also to *production of subjectivity*, or rather subjectification of production as an expression of cognitive labour and of a rise in the quotas of living labour in the relation of production. Thus valorization increases, both in units of value and in the totality of production. The relation between constant capital (command, dead labour) and variable capital (living labour) is radically transformed. Cognitive labour power has asserted itself as more productive – and is subjectively stronger – than industrial labour power ever was.

It thus imposes a radical change on capital itself, not only in the transition from *abstraction* to *extraction* but also in its technical structure, as we have seen. Among the thousands of possible examples, let me take the technologies and the technical composition of *biocapital*. There is plundering of nature and bodies here, but one also finds a rich circulation of medical knowledge, a monopolistic concentration of research, subordination to it of the public organization of health services, and, furthermore, a continuous increase in life expectancy (along with thousands of other antagonistic compositions of biopower); and all these constitute in the end a machine set up for the development of a biomedical project for the governance of health that is, simultaneously, capitalist despotism over nature and natural goods, appropriation of cultural and public goods, and production of subjective devices for the production of a biopolitical common.[2] The same can be said of the technologies of digital capital. There too, each algorithm extracts value from the cognitive labour that is monopolized by the large media structures; but at the same time it has to deal with the irreducible knowledge power [*potenza*] of the operators, who are the real assemblers and builders of the algorithms.[3] The political problem arises at this level. How can the extraction process be challenged, resisted, blocked? We should remember that the juridical categories of property (private and public) are legitimizing figures for the capitalist appropriation of the common. And yet we also remember that the processes of privatizing the common are extremely fragile, given that the relations of power in the mode of production of the common have changed. Faced with a capital forced into a relationship of production that is discontinuous and antagonistic, the power of cognitive and cooperative work produces continuous alternatives.

The first weak point of the capitalist command is created by the affirmation of the autonomous power of productive cooperation, that is, by the virtual hegemony of collective labour vis-à-vis command. Note that today cooperative and cognitive work constitutes a truly singular mass, before which capitalist command vacillates: a mass made up of a multitude of singularities. Whereas capitalist command over the mass was consolidated in the industrial process of production, dominion over the multitude and the pursuit of the singularities that constitute it represents an indefinite horizon, and sometimes an insoluble problem for capital. The paradox consists in the fact that, in cognitive capitalism, production requires a multitude of singularities (because productivity resides in them). Singularization, subjectivation and productivity constitute the 'inside' or the 'against' that the working class of today sets against constant capital, against the boss (and it does so not only as variable capital but as a multitude, as an ensemble of singularities, of linguistic and cooperative networks). Hence the continuous fragmentation of the process, hence the radical difficulties of command, hence the crisis of the institutions of representative democracy, born as they are in a material constitution still determined by the mechanisms of abstraction of values and control that characterized industrial society.

A second weak point consists in the fact that cognitive living labour continuously reappropriates fixed capital, the instruments of labour, and productive knowledge. In this way the technical composition of cognitive living labour is continually enriched and increasingly tilts the capital relation in its favour. (On this topic – the appropriation of fixed capital by living labour – I take the liberty of referring readers to Michael Hardt and Antonio Negri's, *Assembly*, 2017).

New resistances to the capitalist appropriation of the common appear inside these weak points. Obviously I cannot cover all of them here, but I can list a few dispositifs of action that have begun to develop:

(a) first of all, democratic practices of appropriation and management of 'common goods';
(b) insistence, in trade union, fiscal and political negotiations, on the recognition of the common as a basis of the social reproduction of labour; and insistence on the entrepreneurial skills of the singularities put to work. The struggles over welfare go in this direction, and in this case resistance behaviours take on entrepreneurial and alternative qualities;
(c) new measures of the common, which finally begin to be proposed in the quest for new coins whose value is established not by reference to capital's command but as a measure of social needs. The demand for a guaranteed income and the development of alternative currencies are often articulated from this perspective.

To conclude, when the common is removed from capitalist accumulation and valorization, it appears open to the *use* of the multitude. It can then be relegated to an administrative regulation of a democratic and participatory character. The important thing is to recognize the common as a *mode of production* in our society and as a fundamental product of *the work of all*. At this point, the private appropriation of the common is not something that the commune of worker-citizens wish for.

5
The Law of the Common*

Dissolvings

Experts in law have highlighted some fundamental characteristics of global governance: the tendency of governance processes and practices to extend outside of the rigidity of legal systems and regulatory structures; the fragmentation of legal systems under the pressure of conflicts in the global system; and the collision between different kinds and species of laws. Governance† renders vain any attempt to unify global legal systems; rather there is a need to operate a modular logic with which to manage conflicts and ensure the juridical compatibility of the fragments of the global world. In this sense, governance is effectively a government of the state of exception (obviously in the opposite sense to that theorized by Schmitt when he defined sovereignty).

It seems to me that this conclusion is correct and that in the globalized world the deconstruction of traditional forms of law and sovereignty is unavoidable. In short, we have to accept that global governance is 'post-democratic' in that it no longer relies on the apparatus of the representative system that has supported and guaranteed the legitimacy of the state; in that the bodies, techniques and practices of governance possess the flexibility and fluidity necessary to adapt constantly to changing situations; and in that its enforceability is attributable to a plurality of forms of

---

* First presented as 'Il diritto del commune' at the Euronomade 2.0 conference and IUC–Turin seminar, 10 March 2011.
† 'Governance' in English in the original.

regulation controlled, often indirectly, by oligarchies, in particular the economic ones.

OK. But this analysis of the crisis of law and sovereignty in globalization, with the strong deconstructionist content that characterizes it, does not take into account the other term that (contemporaneously, if not synchronously) needs to be addressed in the context of globalization: the theme of the common.

We should note first that 'global' and 'common' are not coextensive as terms. When they are viewed as such, they are vulgarized (Nancy, Esposito etc.). On the contrary: whatever the political and legal overlaps, 'global' is a spatial term, while 'common' is a term related to production with a strong and significant impact at the level of ontology. So why examine them in the same frame? Is it because globalization is the cause of this transition? Of course, it is such in a primary sense, but that does not make it a defining dispositif, much less a dispositif of constitution of the common. Indeed, globalization is a motor of chaotic fragmentations and unpredictable connections, which are often still determined by residual yet effective flows of sovereign action.

Assuming that we don't take an ideological approach, we can perhaps suppose that the term 'common' enters the discussion as a central theme when, in globalization and in the juridical practices that accompany it, we see as a definitional sign a weakening of the transcendentals of private law and public law and of their associated legal practices. It seems that there are aspects, dimensions, profiles of the common that, while not providing an answer to that crisis, requalify the terrain. I shall return to this question later. Let us therefore ask ourselves: at a time when there is a dissolving, not only jurisprudential but also conceptual, of the categories of the old system of law, how is the theme of the common situated?

History

The majority view is that the old right* [*diritto*] is essentially defined on the basis of the concept of private property. Is it not possible to go beyond this horizon? And more, given the dissolutions that take place in a global governance of right, how is the permanence of right to be configured? No matter from what perspective you develop a historical

---

* Or 'system of law'.

analysis around this topic, it seems confirmed that behind the dissolvings that globalization has brought about there are episodes that reveal, through their current crisis, that it is impossible for private law and public right to evolve towards another kind of right, towards a third kind [*tertium genus*], let alone explicitly towards a right based on the common [*diritto del commune*]. It should be added immediately that here the term 'right' is as equivocal and problematic as the term 'common'.

This is confirmed first of all when we consider continental law. In the West, the juridical dimension became fundamental from the moment when it was articulated around the figure of the property-owning individual. The institutional and conceptual framework of western law finds its roots in the needs of individuals – modelled as they are in the conflictual (zero-sum) relationships they have with their procedural counterparts. The establishment of Justinian's *Corpus iuris* serves as the epilogue of a juridical evolution in the Roman world that gave rise to two thousand years of subsequent juridical history. After that, Roman law was to be taken up and redeveloped according to the needs of nascent capitalism, and here it works to interpret and organize appropriately the primitive accumulation of capital. Characteristic of this history is that legal, procedural and jurisprudential procedures consolidate the right of the individual owner and produce a uniform mechanism of validation for property – the market – and for sovereignty – the state. Both these systems produce a concentration of power in the individual and exclude any other decision-making subject in the given jurisdiction. *Hic Rhodus, hic salta* [Here is Rhodes; jump here]. In this context, to seek a transition beyond the strictly privatistic conception of the law and its procedures of application and verification would be in vain. Consequently, seeking a definition of the common in this area is entirely inappropriate. Continental law does not allow for the recognition of the common, no matter how interpreted. For the moment, the frontiers of the zero-sum conflict in the public and private sectors leave no room for the definition of a third pole.

The same conceptual void arises when one follows the tradition of old English law called 'right of common'[*] – which could be translated as right 'to' the common. This is the archaic system of law closely tied to the municipal structures of medieval cities. When Maitland and Pollock analyse this right to the common, they recognize that, far

---

[*] 'right of common' in English in the original.

from being a right 'of' the common, it is an individual right, a right that does not break with juridical individualism, by which I mean with proprietary interest. Indeed, it is a right that the individual can oppose to a collective government of the commons, a right that can in no way lead the need of the common back to the need of equality in the coproduction of non-state legal norms – as the right of common [*il diritto del comune*] has recently been formally defined. It is no coincidence that those ancient definitions of the common were adopted in the 1950s, for example by Hayek, and we know perfectly well in what direction they were taken.

It therefore seems that it is very difficult to recognize a legal system of the common that arises from within the old juridical structures and emancipates itself from them. And it is even more difficult if one thinks, as is often theorized by juridical socialism, that the evolution of public law, which is in an antagonistic relation to private law, may offer a basis for the transition to the law of the common. In this regard, the reference to the Soviet experience is interesting. Evgeny Pašukanis, the greatest jurist of the Soviet era, saw this immediately with great clarity. There is no such thing as proletarian law, he declares; once the transition to developed socialism is accomplished, the disappearance of the categories of bourgeois law will indicate extinction of the law as a whole, or the gradual disappearance of the juridical moment in the relations between people. As for the Soviet state, it is defined as proletarian state capitalism. According to Pašukanis, in proletarian state capitalism there are two realities of exchange and law. One is an economic life that takes place according to 'public' modalities (general programmes, production and distribution plans, etc.); the other is an interconnection between economic units that carry out their activity in the form of the value of circulating goods, and therefore in the legal form of the contract. Now it is evident that the first tendency (that of public law and planning) does not involve any progressive perspective and opens only to a gradual general extinction of the juridical form, translating it into the economic management of society. The second tendency is the one that could develop towards the common, by taking up the autonomy of economic forms and considering them in their cooperation.

It is interesting to note how the impossibility of extracting the law of the common from public law is underlined in the Soviet discourse – minoritarian, but correct from a Marxist point of view – of someone like Pašukanis; that discourse considers instead the possibility of playing on the cooperation of collective labour not only as an exit from proprietary law but as a construction of new forms of non-capitalist life and social organization (Arrighi's Chinese, peasant-based and common-based market without capitalism is a model with the same resonances).

And does our present history, the one in which the procedures of governance are asserting themselves, give us any positive indication on the path towards the common? Is it possible to glimpse in the procedures of governance a tendency towards decentring that opposes the strong tendency towards global concentration of capitalist power, towards fragmentation of powers instead of retention of their solid economic unity, towards the possibility of a diffuse control exercised by an active public opinion, towards an experimentation from below of mechanisms of participation in the social division of labour and in the redistribution of the product? With a lot of optimism, one could perhaps conjecture all this; but with realism it's clear that there is a lot of utopia in the model of a governance conceived of as an exercise of power and production of legal norms, as an open, flexible, institutional modality with a variable geometry, in a juridical programme that has no centre and is left to mechanisms of conflict between norms and of competition between legal systems. And it's clear that our current history shows rather the impossibility of a linear development of the current juridical systems towards the common.

Factual considerations

Given what has been said so far, it remains to ask why the global evokes the common. It evokes it because globalization immediately puts us before what we might call a 'bad' common: the common of capital. The transformations of the law of value – when the temporal measure of labour is replaced by the power of cooperation, and the mechanisms of the circulation of goods, productive services and communication come to be agents of capitalist valorization; when the process of real subsumption happens, that is, the transition from industrial production of commodities to control of a social life made to work through productive automation and computerization – well, all this presents capital as a global biopower. The new basis on which exploitation is established involves a gradual transition of capitalist command from the factory (the Fordist organization of industry and the disciplining of the Taylorized working mass) to the whole of society (through productive hegemony over immaterial labour, valorization through cognitive labour, financial control, etc.). This means that the new basis on which capital operates is the exploitation of cooperation, languages and common social relations (generally it depends on so-called social externalities, internalized into capitalist production on a global scale).

Here is just one example, taken from the current global economic crisis. Many readings of it have been proposed. In any case, whether they came from the right or from the left, the reasons for the crisis have been linked to a separation between finance and 'real production'. If we take on board the new conditions discussed so far, which express the emergence of a new 'common' quality of living labour and its exploitation as such, we have to say that the financialization of the global economy is not an unproductive or parasitic deviation of increasing shares of surplus value and collective savings, but rather a new form of capital accumulation, symmetrical to the new processes of social and cognitive production of value. There is no point in deluding oneself that the answer to getting out of this crisis can avoid building new rights of social ownership of common goods; and these rights are obviously opposed to the right of private property and require a break from that system of public law that represents the legal force of private property. (To repeat what I have elaborated upon in the Uninomade seminars, if until now access to a common good has taken the form of private debt (and it is precisely around the accumulation of this debt that the crisis has exploded), from now on it is legitimate to claim the same right in the form of a social rent. Having these common rights recognized is the only way – and the only right way – to get out of the crisis.)

Approaches 1

So then: traditional law fails to define, or even address, the common. In the current crisis, it is always forced to an action of governance that is, so to speak, restrictive and condemned to substantial ambiguity. In reality, governance can do no more than render social exchange fluid and optimize the fluidity of flows. This means transcribing sovereignty into the language of negotiation, de-hierarchicizing the structures of decision-making, introducing a perspective of fragmented and polycentric relationships, and weakening the traditional separation between public and private; but it can do no more than this. As Chignola reminds us, following in the footsteps of John Fortescue and Judge Coke, from its very beginning the term 'governance' refers both to the government – to the prince's personal right of command and to the hierarchy of administrative offices that depend on him

– and to the dense set of laws, customs, statutes and liberties that characterize the 'intertwining' of rights and powers in a political–civil organization. The setting sun of the state of right rehearses the lights of dawn.

As we alleviate the suspicion with which governance has been treated so far, let us admit, though, that in constituent terms it can open up beyond the conditions in which it currently operates. Let us assume that the terrain of the common appears closer to us, as a terrain of transition from the public to the common, and that governance adapts to it by traversing the narrative plot of this transition. The question to ask at this point could be: if traditional right is not able to define (control, transcribe, institute) the common, how can governance approach it? Which is to say: will it be governance that will construct the new system of law – ambiguously, expressing a sort of *conatus*?

Approaches 2

From a reflexive point of view, or from the point of view of the philosophy of right, we can try to raise the problem of how to define the common. I offer here some examples that represent extreme cases (there are infinite combinations among them), but that could perhaps help us to advance.

So the common has been defined at one end in the language of a sociopolitical Darwinism, as the effect of economic–political relations of coproduction. Along this line, we know the famous formula of Saint Simon embraced by Marx and Engels, in which the administration of things will take the place of the government of humans. Here the common appears as the economic administration of society by itself. To the self-balancing of interests that the liberal market proposes, socialism responds with the conscious economic self-organization of people. This formula recurs all the time in socialism, at least up to Lenin. It is obviously a teleology of the common, built on industrial technological rationality. The common is a fact [*fatto*], participle of the verb 'to do', 'make' [*fare*] – a real movement that abolishes the present state of things.[*]

---

[*] This is a paraphrase of the famous definition of communism in *The German Ideology*: 'We call communism the *real* movement which abolishes the present state of things.' Karl Marx and Friedrich Engels, *The German Ideology*, ed. C. J. Arthur, London: Lawrence and Wishart, 1970, pp. 56–7.

An opposite model of definition of the common is sociological–institutional. The development from civil society to forms of public organization and to a common conceived of as a corporate or associative outcome is seen precisely as the product of a continuous activity. The economic and technological necessity of the first model is here opposed to a procedural and social activism. Examined in its most recent figurations, the 'institutional' common is defined (for example by Luc Boltanski) by abandoning sociologies that emphasize the vertical dimensions and opacity of the actors' alienated consciousness in favour of a sociology that stresses horizontal relationships (and, obviously, networks) and in situ performance from actors guided by strategic motivations or moral needs. The elements of performativity of the social are brought to the fore and, when also the public (the state) is evoked and assumed to be a balancing element in the processes, this pragmatic sociological institutionalism recognizes both the contradictions in which the process is locked in this way and the power of its open dispositifs. In short, a real movement that acts on the present state of things.

A third interesting model (which represents a median between the two extremes), still with a view to a definition of the common, is the philosophical return of a weak dialectical theory of relationship. Habermas's formalism advanced on this path, and Honneth's realism proceeds on it too. The common is seen here as a (weak) *Aufhebung* without necessity; the difficulty of realizing it consists in determining the co-possibility of differences in the indefinite framework of conditions. We experience here, among other things, the difficulties that are now evident in the development of the Foucauldian project when we consider it as an epistemological model rather than as a political dispositif.

These approaches remain just that. All attack the idea that the common can be somehow presupposed, and all affirm that we can think only of social practices of production of the common. How will governance be able to interpret these premises and possibly go beyond, on a path that leads to the common?

In order to avoid further obstacles, we can ask ourselves whether, when we proceed further on this terrain, the common determination of acting in common must necessarily take the form of an 'institution'. Responding negatively to that question, one can say that the production of rules that do not have the quality of law can take the form of producing negotiated usages, of practices of the common that can arise only through concrete determinations and relations of power. In this context one may further ask: how can one articulate the terrain of ownership with that of uses? What are the conditions of co-possibility of individuals and singularities? How is it possible to prevent the solidity of identities from foreclosing any possibility of the co-presence of singularities? What are the processes of subjectivation that traverse these constitutive processes? Could the constitution of a commune that is not 'additive' and not even 'integrative', of a commune that is not a 'sum' and not even an 'organism', arise from a dialectical progression (or regression, strong or tenuous) that has a Hegelian stamp?

To answer this question, let me introduce some further questions and experiments.

Experiment 1

If we assume that the context of governance in which the plurality of actors develops its action lacks any determination of finality or value, and if every determination is a power [*potenza*] that wins (or loses) vis-à-vis other powers, the first juridical example that can be adduced in the search for the common is the one traditionally represented by the international law system of war. Here the common paradoxically reconnects with the global. It is certainly a terrain free of formalisms. In fact, if one attempted to operate in this area with the liberal concepts of rule of law [*Stato di diritto*], or with doctrines of justice anchored in the abstract schemes of metaphysical rationalism, one would run obvious risks. But by doing so one reduces juridical practice to the mere recording of fact, which is how sociology and realistic empiricism proceed; one enters an area – labelled by Carl Schmitt, for international law, as non-law – where governance is defined in the absence of any possibility of *nomos*. We are once again immersed in dissolution. The experiment of international law does not change the dissolutions, it only shifts them. Here a new reflection must be made on the terrain of globalization – a reflection that recognizes the basic antagonisms between which the process of global reorganization is moving, in every sense; a reflection that eliminates any homology with the past, any reference to the old international constitutions; a reflection that seeks to build provisional and effective regulations in new spaces and on new themes – biopolitical, media-related, and especially financial.

A second example is that of trade union law in the class struggle. In the transition to post-Fordism and in the course of the economic crisis, as the German labour compromise and generally industrial contractualism (more or less corporative) collapsed, the problem of the regulation of social labour and that of the redistribution of the gross domestic product have been freed from any juridical conditioning, displaced from the terrain of direct production to that of social production. In this case, too, any homology with past trade union law is empty; again, a constituent initiative is to be opened. But in this case, too, the terrain is characterized by determinations similar to those defined by international law – a true disaster of traditional juridical forms. For the moment, only tactical operations of resistance seem possible.

Experiment 2

This is the line of *Commonwealth*. It leads us to tackle the problem of a possible system of law of the common from the point of view of the ontology of the common.

This path starts with the recognition of the construction and functional subjugation of the common by global, financial and military capitalism. Far from proposing processes of pure recognition or appropriation of the structures and figures of the 'communism of capital' and its state, this line proposes to think of the processes of governance as tools for a further destructuring of traditional law and, second, gives itself the objective of calling for the emergence of new figures of productive cooperation in this process of destructuration.

Thus the only way out of these problems seems to be as follows:

(1) The first condition is to repropose the theme of the common on a terrain that is not socially homogeneous, that envisages neither pre-established institutionalization nor homologies, but that is traversed by originary antagonisms: on the one hand there is an increasingly precarious labour power that recognizes its autonomy from capital; on the other hand, there is the relationship of command that capital continually seeks to renew. The solution of these conflicts cannot be given according to any teleological or dialectical determination. One moves in a Machiavellian context. Every determination is a power that wins (or loses) over other powers. The sense of the process is assimilated and produced by the power of collective decision.
(2) In this framework, the common cannot be posited in continuity with the juridical tradition, cannot be configured as a terrain on which ideas of justice are proposed from the outside... it can

contain and build only uses and can govern them in immanence, in their reciprocity and commonality. International law (precisely as non-law) is from this point of view the model we can point to, but in reverse to how Carl Schmitt posed the problem.

(3) The overturning of the Schmittian perspective – not recovery of the 'exception' but insistence on the 'excedence' of cognitive labour – the acceptance of a matching biopolitical context and so on, in short, the study of doctrines and practices that deconstruct western law and the exercise (within the deconstruction of the law) of constituent power, are the only way out that can be followed today in these matters.

In the 1920s Pašukanis had proposed some extremely interesting lines. He was claiming that the logic of juridical concepts corresponds to the logic of the social relations in a society that produces commodities and that the root of private law as a system resides in these relations rather than in permission from authority. Thus the logic of relations of domination and subordination falls only partially under juridical concepts. Consequently the juridical conception of the state can never become a theory and will always remain an ideological alteration of the facts. To imagine a common law [*diritto del commune*] (but why still speak of law?), it will then be necessary, once the property-owning constitution has been destructured, to wind back from plurality, from the network of labour relations, to forms of regulation that take in and develop the potential of social productive relations – and these constitute, in equality and co-production, non-state juridical norms for the regulation of common life.

For example, it will be necessary to follow phenomena of cooperation of labour power, of self-valorization, that introduce a surplus of productive capacity of the single, collective labour power; it will be necessary to explore the set of financial phenomena, revealing from the inside the power of the symmetrical relations between social production and the system of signs – probably reinventing at this level a theory of labour value and of its measure. Only in this case will it be possible to establish lines that, for example, track back from welfare to the common, and not just tactically but strategically, at long last. And in this light the common begins to define itself as an arena of democratic participation plus distributive equality.

6
Federalism and Movements of the Common*

I

1. The contemporary state is in crisis. It seems that the figure that Hobbes inaugurated by giving his account of the state machine has become completely obsolete. The quantity of material processes that characterize our present times spills beyond the outline of that image – in relation to institutions, on the one hand, and, on the other, in relation to subjectivities. The nexus between the form, the material and the power of the state is being thoroughly transformed. The eventual configurations are still undecided but mark a decisive shift, and they reposition the political problem to another level.

As a simple example, take the disarticulation and subsequent rearticulation of the nexus between command, territory and systems of law [*diritti*] brought about by globalization and by the reconfiguration of world spaces. Instead of having a system of international law derived from European public law [*ius publicum europaeum*], we now have spaces defined by globalism; markets that are differentiated within the imperial *unicum*; zones of territorialization of the flows of global investment; global metropolises as nodes of the network that dictates their orientation (transnational and subcontinental areas of influence...); processes of non-state law-making that disturb and stand outside the hierarchies of normative sources and order relations at the planetary level (patent law, a new commercial law [*lex*

---

* First recorded as 'Federalismo e movimenti del comune', outline of a presentation for the summer seminar of Euronomade 2.0, 2014.

mercatoria], the semi-constituent role of private international law); the growing relevance of non-representative powers that marginalize democratic self-determination (the IMF, the European Central Bank); a tendential drop in participation in the electoral or representative process in the mature democracies; disintegration of the relation between territory, national market and state, with accompanying consequences for the *deconstitutionalization* of social rights; the growing prominence of global migrations as lines of flight and of deterritorialization of subjectivity.

The nation state no longer presents itself as the sole determining source of law but clearly appears to be in crisis. As Saskia Sassen has shown, the new and complex 'assemblages' of power, law and territory have now transmuted into a system of global law centred on a multiplicity of partial regimes that answer to the needs of specialized sectors. In the same spirit, Günther Teubner speaks of a 'corporate constitutionalism', in other words of juridical forms expressed by various singular groups in civil society.

Obviously, given all the challenges that face the classical figure of the state form, the theory of federalism is also affected and finds itself having to deal with increasingly deterritorialized and mobile diversities. So we have to raise with extreme clarity the question of how to think about *a federalism beyond the state*. The entire phenomenology of federalism has to be read not merely in structural terms but by privileging its *procedural* dimension: this is in the first place about processes of collective learning that cannot be predetermined by the letter of constitutive pacts but are open to experience and experimentation.

2. Let us now look at this whole dissolutive process from another point of view: I mean, not from the point of view of statute-based law but from that of the constituent powers that emanate from the movements. I am thinking of the great movements of 2011 – not the Arab movements as much as those that developed in Europe and the United States. The critique that these movements have raised against the classical organization of the state is that, given all the phenomena outlined so far, the traditional powers and their separation (within reciprocal control) have been completely transfigured. With this they say nothing that has not been already recognized in part by the constitutionalists. Among US constitutionalists, for instance, there is Bruce Ackerman, who is concerned that the expansion of executive power creates a danger of dictatorship; or Sheldon Wolin, who claims that the dynamic democratic capacities of the American constitution have already been emptied to the point of

creating an 'inverted totalitarianism': while the totalitarian state controls capitalist structures, in inverted totalitarianism the capitalist structures control the structures of the state directly. In Europe even Rosanvallon and Giddens, the fathers of the 'third way', admit now the impossibility of state control over financial power. On the other hand, what do the movements add to this general awareness? They consider republican constitutions, representative practices, and the whole system of powers to be *incapable of reform*, and they begin to propose the first elements of a new constituent power. In this context, the reference to federalism – considered not a pyramidal organization but a *spatial network* – is fundamental to characterizing the new figures of constituent power, in anticipation of any figure of legislative power. It has to be conceived of as the outcome of a real federalism that, by enhancing the plural and procedural dimensions, deconstructs the rigidity between representation (politics, interests, etc.) and organicity (of the administrative, of the executive function, etc.) of the state and reinterprets the dialectic between resistance and participation in an open way. Will it still be possible to recover these 'post-state' virtualities of federalism and to make them the key to a constituent power and to a legislative proposal that does not end up in a perverse and equally powerless centralism, in a renewed Jacobinism? Just as, through the continuity of constituent power, the legislative power seems to adapt to the contemporaneity of social movements, so by adopting a federal structure it will be able to adapt to the (local and diffuse) spatial dimension of the movements. At this point complexity becomes productive: the network will in fact be able to measure its links in relation to the always singular dimensions of legislative governance.*

All this means that, at this point, any movement that sets itself against representation makes proposals that are constituent – as well as being, obviously, destituent. When expressed in this form, the movements press forward new constitutional principles. It should be remembered that in 2011 the constituent thrust preceded the revolt, so to speak; it was intrinsic to the resistance – it governed it and prefigured it. It did not ask that the state turn aside from its monopoly of violence, or that capitalism become good, or that the banks stop speculating; rather it imagined new forms of production and social order.

It is clear that, in contrast to what happened in the 1930s in the face of a crisis of similar intensity, politics is unable to develop a

---

* 'governance' in English in the original.

constituent design capable of providing an adequate solution to the intensity of the economic and social crisis. Neither a Keynes nor a Roosevelt have yet appeared on the scene, and in any case it is hard to see how their recipes, valid for the era of industrial production, could be adapted to the post-industrial era. What this crisis needs is a qualitative leap, a change of paradigm: the current liberal policies do not offer anything at this level. Nor do they propose anything that so much as matches the history of constitutionalism and of modern constitutions. This has always been a history of mediations, built first around mercantile relations of exchange (liberal constitutions) and later around the capital–labour dialectic (welfarist constitutions). Now it is really hard to imagine what mediations can be built around the financialization processes that live at the heart of contemporary capitalism. Categories such as representation and democracy, not to mention national sovereignty, cannot be redefined outside the recognition that the financial and global markets have become the headquarters par excellence of an autonomous production of legality and politics. The command exercised by financial capital tends increasingly to sidestep the institutional mediations of modern democracies and is based on the blackmail made possible by the fact that, in the last resort, the guarantees of enjoying essential rights (from housing to health), and also of wages, depend irreversibly on the dynamics and continuous turbulences of the financial markets.

In this situation, the movements move with unique constituent characteristics. For example, they have an 'alternative temporality'. 'Alternative' is not an action or a purpose or a discourse based on the radical asymmetry of the point from which the alternative will is expressed; *it is another place*. Now, this singular place has an autonomy that makes its functioning coherent in time, producing subjectivities, struggles and constituent principles within a process of independent wills. Temporality is subsumed by this independence – and it is alternative because it is independent. Within this temporality, in the viral expression of the constituent requests, you will find different powers [*potenze*]: not only demands for democracy and freedom, for equality and access to the common, but complex constructions (of knowledge and projects, of generalized expertise*...) and constructions of common ventures.

But you will also find the exercise of counterpower when social needs, economic urgencies or environmental threats require it. The

---

* 'expertise' in English in the original.

American constitutional affirmation of the right of resistance must be assumed here: many struggles, in many far distant places, with protagonists with different styles and forms of life; struggles sometimes to overthrow tyrants, sometimes to denounce poverty, sometimes to destroy or to appropriate goods; struggles whose protagonists sometimes demand the right to vote and free elections, sometimes propagandize abstention and exodus from politics – and so on. How and why might these struggles be seen as expressions of the same cycle? How might we think that they are so original as to break the rigid continuity of the forms of capitalist domination and offer a radical subversion of the democratic model? We live in a plural political world, but a profound homogeneity nevertheless traverses the different forms of struggle and the different places of their onset. The political ontology of global capitalist domination, and the struggles within and against this globality, are undoubtedly a horizon on which variously textured forms and planes of constituent struggles and wills stand out. We are interested in moving through these differences not only to confirm the same foundation (the global world of neoliberalism and of one-way thinking [*pensiero unico*]) but also the common goal in which differences recognize and recompose themselves in the process of struggle and movement.

I have already argued that all these experiences are born inside a laboratory of communication. It seems that their glue is initially informatic, linguistic and cooperative (and it is clear that in all and each of these experiences the hegemony of cognitive labour is a given). I have also noted how this cooperation is built into the slow times of constructing a common language, into the rhythm of a complex spatial diffusion of the messages produced – but most of all of a self-control, a self-limitation, a self-management of political temporality. There should be nothing that has not been decided by consensus: the decision-making of the multitude requires the autonomy of a constructed temporality. It is no coincidence, then, that this autonomous communication of slogans and of militant will enforces its powers of viral diffusion (initially, at least) on small communities and political affinity groups. The Israeli *indignados* camping out in the main streets of Tel Aviv claimed to have rebuilt not only the spirit but also the political form of the old kibbutz. The Spanish *indignados* showed – in their little tent towns, in the commissions that cooperated in the construction of a political programme – how a constituent discourse that moved from below, from the simple and small-scale communication of affects and reasons, could be carried through into general assemblies and there create a decision-making machine.

It is no coincidence that the novelty of these movements and of their constituent proposal tends to find support and a symbol in a renewed model of federalism. Small communities connect and build their unity not in the renunciation but in the integration of differences; thus federalism becomes an engine of recomposition. Obviously we test here the continued existence of very few elements of a theory of the federalist state or sovereignty; nevertheless we find, on the small scale, the strong passions of an associative intelligence that have sustained federalist ideologies on the large scale. Here ideology turns into practice: a practice of resistance. How far and how long this will last no one knows. And yet the resistance is real ... the response of capitalism proves it: to break the federal unity that the movements build in the struggle, capitalism is normally forced to carry out sophisticated operations, which cost the ruling elites a lot (recourse to a religious alternative, Islamic in the case in point, in the countries of the Arab Spring; ferocious repression against the 2011 English riots* and use of racist weapons; provocations concerning the border between violence and non-violence, where the movement has reached a high maturity of association, thanks to Spain and the United States).

A plural ontology of the political: this is the reality in which the initiative of the movements appears and takes place. This pluralism indicates federative cooperation and assembly of struggles that differ in inspiration and in project and a constituent democracy that upholds differences as a terrain for synthesis and further proposals. It is a plurality of movements against global capital, against finance capital, for the reconquest of the common and for the production of a constitution of the common: these things are in our minds by now. But it is important to live them, it is essential to participate in their construction while being aware of it. In the face of a plural ontology of the political we have so far analysed the political and plurality ... now it is necessary to enter the ontological machine. This penetration is not an impossible task: it consists in getting ready for [*disporsi*] the production of subjectivity, becoming its dispositif. Communicating, learning and teaching, studying and communicating, being activists and participating in struggles – such is the dispositif of the production of subjectivity. Militancy constitutes its central axis. A plural ontology of the political finds its synthesis at the intersection and in the recomposition of militant subjectivities.

---

* 'English Riots' in English in the original.

In short, to conclude, this is an example redolent of what I mean by the spatiality of the common: a residing together of bodies. The *indignados* as well as Occupy Wall Street give a full demonstration of this dimension of the common.

The struggles in Val di Susa are a good illustration. They offer clarification on a whole series of elements described thus far:

(a) within–against expertise;
(b) exercise of counterpowers;
(c) democratic decision-making processes (general assemblies, etc.);
(d) elaboration of singular tactics within a general strategy;
(e) attack on institutional representation and possible relegitimization of representatives through struggle, and so on.

II

1. It's time to return to the theories of federalism – of federalism understood as a category of public law. Now, we are acquainted with two traditions of federalism. The first, which is hegemonic, is associated with Pufendorf. It casts federalism as a process of assimilation of local and state differences. It is traversed by the idea of sovereignty and has to deal with the dilemma of Calhoun. In this way the federalist conception slips into the tradition and difficulties of sovereignty. Olivier Beaud sees federalism as being a form of the state.

At the other end is the conception of Althusius (and partly of Harrington). This conception treats the federal constitution, or rather the federalist model, as another way of thinking about politics, as a dualism of power: on the one hand, sovereign power; on the other, the powers that are subject but always resistant, locally determined. In the Althusian view, the form of federation appears as a dialectic of sovereignty against resistance and participation, and this relationship is considered as a 'dualistic ellipse'. How, then, can we imagine a government whose necessity derives precisely from the radical and irrepressible plurality of the political entity? We can try stepping into a horizon of radical criticism of democracy. We must abandon here the idea that the identity of the rulers and the governed must live as a regulative idea in the constitutional organization of the government function. While in the conception of legitimate power the citizens are totally submissive because the power to be obeyed is understood as a power of all, in Althusius' conception plurality persists as a political and constitutional factor before the government and thus guarantees continuity in the political action of the governed. Government is therefore possible only as the product of a dualism of power.

2. But beware. If we look at this process within a biopolitical condition, that is, in a place where the genealogy of the function of government is closely linked to the genealogy of the economy, several difficulties arise. In the twentieth-century welfare state, citizens are no longer evaluated as simple, private legal entities, collectively recomposed through political representation, but are reclassified as portions of the population – and such reclassification requires other knowledge and social planning. In this context, federalism risks becoming functional to neoliberal governmentality all over again. Biopolitics, when we talk about it in connection to a government function that carries out its regulatory action in territorialized areas, is certainly open to a challenge against those who resist; but this challenge can always be bent to the functional exigencies of command. How, then, can the Althusian point of view be reaffirmed, on the one hand against the functional degeneration of governance and, on the other, in the face of the countertendency of local parties to shut themselves into populist or identitarian positions?

What resists the dispositifs of sovereignty and escapes the classic forms of representation is freedom: a freedom that, as the alternative face of subjection to governance processes, configures other needs and other desires in biopolitics. It seeks to install other forms of life. If the new technologies of power organize themselves with a view to capturing and governing a freedom no longer related to the state but constantly in excess and centrifugal, we find ourselves facing the perpetual dissident. 'Perpetual dissidents' are those citizens who do not direct their desire for security and order to their own sovereign but are determined to be governed as little as possible and to govern themselves as much as possible.

Is it possible to recognize in the instances of federalism today the expression of a radical tendency to exodus, the trace of authentic lines of flight, a radical tendency of political subjectivation around claims[*] that cannot be prosecuted via the filter of representation? In this context, what are the cooperative networks of cognitive capitalism's general intellect,[†] the form of accumulation within which the production and control of knowledge become the fundamental stake

---

[*] 'claims' in English in the original.
[†] Here and passim, 'general intellect' in English in the original.

in the valorization of capital? How do the social times necessary for the constitution of knowledge – crucial nodes in the valorization of production – aggregate when these powers tend more and more to overflow the boundaries of individual companies? Here federalism begins by presenting itself as an elusive reality in the network, in the common.

3. This doesn't leave us with much in our hands... but we have some leads. Thus far I have worked on the constituent temporality of the common; the discussion of federalism then led to a discussion of spatiality, to the spatial figure of the common, which constituent language must make its own.

So let me return to the concept of federalism, privileging the procedural dimension, as I have already said, and thus casting it in political forms appropriate to the common. Let me refer in particular to a work by Daniel Elazar, who sees the category of federation as a process and not as a formal fact.[1] Elazar's most important contribution is thus the emphasis he places on the fact that federalism organizes its political space in the structure of a *matrix*, thereby radically distancing himself from the pyramidal criterion on which is based the historical and theoretical model of the modern state form. The main experiences of 'real federalism' actually involve a hierarchy, a pyramid of governments with gradations of power that flow from the top down or from a centre to the periphery. But what I want to emphasize here is that the matrix structure of the federal political space evokes the image (and the reality) of the network, which in the great transformation of recent decades has established itself as a dominant figure, both in the field of new communication technologies and in that of the organization of work and commerce, both in the analysis of new governance processes and in that of the powers that organize the old and new 'global cities' – to give just a few examples.

It is clear that, when analogies of this type (e.g. between federalism and network) are made, it is difficult to draw from them a thought concerning the potentials and the contemporary horizons of *a federalism beyond the state*. In such cases there is a permanent risk of slipping into ideology and utopianism. Terms such as solidarity, subsidiarity and communication risk not being materially qualified. But more than anything we risk forgetting that the financialization processes have made possible, at least since the crisis of the early 1970s, a formidable non-centralized concentration of power. In other words they have made it possible to compensate at the level of power and strategic decision for that very strong decentralization that has characterized the great transformation undergone by the capitalist mode of production in recent decades, and has done so both intensively (in the area of human qualities and skills valorized by capital) and extensively (territorially and spatially).

By saying this I seem, again, to throw into doubt all the premises from which my discussion of the dynamic and procedural nature of federalism started. Here are the questions. What forms can the control of the power of finance take, and in what spatial coordinates? Is a constitutionalization of this power generally possible? How should we think about a reappropriation of the immense wealth 'frozen' in financial incomes, and how should we then answer these questions as we traverse federalist thinking? It is clear that the only answer that can be given to these questions is one that reopens the game of counterposed forces. Federalism, interpreted as I have interpreted it, can allow us to broaden the field of contestation and to extend the guerrilla warfare for the reappropriation of the common.

7

Disarticulating Ownership?

Common Goods and the Possibilities of Law*

Let me begin by recalling a brief passage in the young Marx:

> Work is the living foundation of private property, private property as a creative source of itself. Private property is nothing but objectified labour. If, then, one wants to give private property a fatal blow, it must not be attacked only as an objective *condition*, but as an *activity*, as labour. It is one of the biggest misunderstandings to speak of free human and social work, of work *without* private property. Hence abolition of private property comes to reality only when it is conceived of as abolition of work, an abolition that naturally becomes possible only through work, that is, through the material activity of society.[1]

Marx adopts here, from the Lockean tradition, the 'classic' definition of private property, secular and liberal. This is the very definition of possessive individualism.[2] As we know, Macpherson has made an extensive study of possessive individualism. From this perspective, individuals were considered free insofar as they owned their own person and their own capacities; human essence consisted in not depending on the will of others and liberty was a function of what one possessed as an individual. (This view was not very different, incidentally, from Harrington's and Winstanley's conception of freedom; and I am happy to refer to these authors because the collective telos of their reasoning incentivised a communist project.)

So then, society consists of relations of exchange between property owners. Political society becomes a machine designed to defend

---

* First presented as 'Disarticolare la proprietà? Beni comuni e possibilità del diritto' at the Faculty of Law of the University of Perugia, 8 October 2013.

private property and maintain an orderly relationship in matters of exchange. If we broaden our gaze and place Hobbes, as Macpherson rightly does, at the theoretical centre of possessive individualism, where it is developed in universal terms, we are in position to appreciate the definition of individual freedom elaborated by him with great rigour – and consequently the definition of property as the economic translation of freedom itself: 'The Value, or Worth of a man, is as of all other things, his Price; that is to say, so much as would be given for the use of his Power...'[3]

But we know how profoundly work has changed today with respect to the definition of possessive individualism. The question is, will the concept of private property change too? Or rather in what sense, in what direction should we transform the critique of property? In order to answer, let us first take a look at how work or labour changes; and, to avoid simple-minded references to Italian critical sources (which in Italy are always tiresome, God knows why), let us reread Robert Castel, Manuel Castells[4] and countless others, well summarized by Luc Boltanski and Eve Chiappello in a book that draws a conclusive analysis of the new forms of productive labour today.[5] Labour is realized and valorized in a world where the visibility of communication networks and information connections is continuously growing; consequently people work nowadays in ever more flexible and mobile arrangements, which are precarious from the angle of payment – and the world of work is increasingly marked by indeterminacy of times and spaces, by anxiety and by anomie. As for the creation of value, it takes place in cooperative flows where languages and affects are subsumed under the material processes of production, and labour – what we call variable capital – is very frequently interchangeable with machinery – what we call fixed capital. In other words, the quality of labour is progressively marked by singular figures that combine to cooperate with constant capital, since they autonomously appropriate fractions or times, or uses or functions of fixed capital. Thus work has changed radically from the way it was described and stood ontologically in the age of possessive individualism. So then: have the forms of the relationship between activity and property also changed radically? Of course. What remains, then, ontologically speaking, of the concept of private property?

It is worth pointing out that it is not the first time that such changes have occurred: already in the industrial age (that is, when the archaeology of original accumulation fades and the hegemony of large-scale industry is imposed, with modernity) there had been a major change in the relationship between labour and private property. Gradually the entrepreneurial and managerial theories of industry had shifted the concept of ownership towards a function of management. Early twentieth-century American realism charted these changes very clearly.

With the latest modification, as indicated by Boltanski, the transformation of the concept of property (insofar as it connects to the transformation of work) becomes ontologically extreme and a purely ideological survival; and it is not clear why the definitive obsolescence of the Hobbesian definition (and, partly, of the Marxian one) is not recognized. However, one should stress the insuperable advantage that the Marxian discourse shows over the Hobbesian, if only in overcoming its concept of labour. In fact Marx not only holds tight the ideas of freedom and property but also connects the idea of labour with that of property by giving the concept of property a dynamic reading, and in this way allows us to move well beyond possessive individualism. So let us, in our turn, proceed further on the terrain of defining property, bearing in mind the Marxian labour–property equation.

So then: the change in the world of labour for which I cited Boltanski fundamentally renews the concept of private property. It appears on an ambiguous terrain, where the elements of material and immaterial activity (physical and intellectual labour), the individual and social dimensions, and the singular and cooperative qualities are confusedly interchanged in processes of production (and all the more in processes of exploitation) and where, as I have stated, even portions of fixed capital are from time to time appropriated by labour power or snatched (extracted) from the bosses' command over the metamorphosis of productive labour. Furthermore, independent processes of subjectification function within these transitions of capitalist accumulation, inducing in them unique excedences and innovations.

At this point one has to wonder whether the concept of private property still makes sense ontologically. In reality, the relationship between labour and property seems to be constituted in the network society now, when the walls of the factory give way, when work tends to reconfigure itself as a service relationship, when productive connections are expanded in the metropolis, when value is extracted at the entire social–productive level: in such a situation private property seems to have become a contingent concept, devoid of necessity. It is in fact money, and thus financial capital and public action, that seem to establish here any relationship between labour and command (property?).

A new property convention is thus created, and the rule of finance is imposed here to redefine ownership. It is the possession of money – the financial convention – that is established as the regulating norm of social and productive activities and in consequence as access to a 'proprietary reality' whose conceptual confusion does not detract from its effectiveness. Property becomes paper-based, monetary or share, movable or real estate; it has a conventional and juridical nature. André Orléan and Christian Marazzi have usefully highlighted this transformation.[6] This is about considering the financial convention as a command that is independent of any ontological determination: the convention establishes and consolidates a 'proprietary sign' in terms of 'private property' (see in particular Heinsohn and Steiger),[7] and it holds fast even when it appears as a crisis, as excess – and not just vis-à-vis the old and static determinations of labour value but especially in relation to that continuous anticipation and increment that characterize its dealings with the financial capture of socially produced value and its operations towards its extension at the global level.

Let me make it clear, then, that in this new configuration of the property regime the material basis of the law of value remains. Nevertheless, we are not dealing here with individual labour that becomes abstract, but with immediately social and common labour, directly exploited by capital. The rule of finance can be posited hegemonically, because in the new mode of production the *common* has emerged as an eminent power [*potenza*], as the substance of the relations of production, and is invading the entire social space as a norm of valorization. Financial capital pursues this extension of profit, tries to anticipate it, presses on movable and real estate rent and anticipates them as financial rent. As Harribey puts it in discussion with Orléan, if value does not appear here in substantial terms, it does not look like a simple accounting phantasmagoria either: it is the sign of a productive common, mystified but effective, which develops more and more intensively and extensively.[8]

So, rather than talking about the social function of property, it would perhaps be better to speak of the social properties of labour, since the social function of property seems to have flowed back towards capital, to the point of configuring itself as its financial figure. We are immersed in that structure, which is enveloping but also highly chaotic.

Only the recognition of the social properties of labour can change this picture. But we cannot consider them without first attempting to unravel a series of paradoxes that the current condition of capitalist development proposes. Which paradoxes? What do I mean by paradoxes? I mean contradictions that are difficult to overcome in this chaotic environment. They are subjected to exceptional forms of governance,* in the attempt, always critically unresolved, to restore conceptual equilibrium and functional effectiveness.

Now, a first paradox regards *production* and consists in the fact that financial capitalism represents the most abstract and detached form of command, even as it concretely invests the entirety of life. The 'reification' of life and the 'alienation' of subjects are created by a productive command that, in the new mode of production organized by financial capital, has become completely transcendent – a productive command over a cognitive workforce that nevertheless turns out to be autonomously productive when it is obliged to produce surplus value, precisely because the latter is cognitive, immaterial, creative, and not immediately consumable.

The paradox is completely clear when we consider that, as production is essentially based on social cooperation (whether in information technology, in care work, in the service sector, or elsewhere), the valorization of capital comes into conflict not simply with the massification of variable capital but with the resistance and autonomy of a multitude that has reappropriated for itself a portion of fixed capital (thus presenting itself, if you like, as a 'machinic subject') and a continuous 'relative' ability to organize networks of social labour. This paradox and contradiction very violently counterpose constant capital (in its financial form) and variable capital (in the hybrid form it assumes once it has incorporated fixed capital) – and therefore tendentially implement the verticalization of command.

The second paradox is that of *property*. Private property (what we define juridically as such) tends to be subjected more and more to the figures of rent. Rent arises today essentially from processes of monetary circulation that take place in the services of financial capital and of real estate capital – or from processes of valorization that take place in industrial services.

Now, when (private) goods present themselves as services, when capitalist production is valorized essentially through services, private property blurs its traditional characteristics of 'possession' and appears rather as command over (and exploitation of) the cooperation that constitutes those services and makes them productive.

For what we call public powers [*poteri pubblici*], this is the source

---

* 'governance' in English in the original.

of an urgency to manifest themselves as sovereign powers [*poteri sovrani*] in an extreme, transcendent manner, in order to restore to private property the value-creating [*valorifica*] and legal (juridical) function that the transformation of social production tends to remove from it. However, in post-industrial societies the public mediation of class relations becomes increasingly difficult, because sovereignty itself has been privatized – patrimonialized by finance capital – for the same reason why private property has dissolved: it is no longer a possession, it is the use of a service. Thus the sovereign public [*il pubblico sovrano*] clashes now not with corporations, trade unions, or collective bodies of labour (which represented themselves as private subjects, too), but with the cooperation and social circulation of figures that continually compose and recompose themselves in material production and in cognitive production: in short, with what we call the 'common'. So what destroys the institution of public property is not exclusively the progressive 'private patrimonialization' of public goods but also the ontological dynamic that this phenomenon sets in motion after the dissolution of the private – in other words the continuous drift of public management towards emergency, the slippage of emergency into corruption, and the destruction of the common through the power of exception.

The sovereign public now stands only in a paradoxical way, or rather it dissolves in the face of the common, which emerges precisely within processes of social production and valorizing cooperation. Insofar as it still features, the sovereign public is a pure mystification of the common.

The third paradox is one that biocapital confirms in its confrontation with *the bodies of workers*. Here the clash, the contradiction and the antagonism are fixed when, in the post-industrial phase, in the era in which cognitive capital becomes hegemonic, capital is obliged to put human bodies directly into production, making them become machines so that they cease to be just labour commodities. Thus, in the new processes of production, bodies become specialized and gain autonomy with increasing efficacy, so that, through the resistance and struggles of the machinic labour power, the demand for a production of humans for humans [*dell'uomo per l'uomo*] – that is, for the human being as a living machine – develops more and more explicitly.

At the moment when workers reappropriate a part of fixed capital and present themselves, in variable and often chaotic manner, as cooperating actors in the processes of value creation, as precarious yet autonomous subjects in the valorization of capital, a complete inversion occurs in the function of labour in relation to capital: workers stop being just the instrument that capital uses to conquer nature – which means, trivially, producing goods. Having incorporated the tools, having metamorphosed anthropologically, and having regained use value, they act rather machinically, in an alterity and autonomy from capital that they want to make total. The class struggle that we can now call 'biopolitical' is situated between this objective tendency and the practical dispositifs in the constitution of these machinic workers.

All these three paradoxes remain unresolved in the action of capital. Consequently, the stronger the resistance, the harsher the state's attempt to restore power. Every act of resistance is thus condemned as an illegal exercise of counterpower; every manifestation of revolt is defined as devastation and pillage. Another paradox (and this time it is pure mystification) is that, in exercising maximum violence, capital and its state need to appear as inevitable and neutral figures: maximum violence is exercised by instruments and by 'technical' bodies. As Thatcher proclaimed, 'there is no alternative'.

How do we act politically within these paradoxes? Confronting the paradox of production means, fundamentally, developing self-valorization and reappropriating, progressively and more and more decisively, the fixed capital employed in social production processes. So it means resistance, self-valorization and appropriation, as against the multiplication of operations of capture and privatization that begins to develop. Reappropriating fixed capital means building a 'common' – a common against the capitalist appropriation of life, a common as development of civic and political uses, as capacity of management. Knowledge and income are the objectives that fundamentally qualify the cognitive proletariat; these are right from the start political objectives just as much as the wage increase was for the industrial worker. In Rosa Luxemburg's words,

> The struggle against the reduction of relative wages [and thus, today, for a social income] also means struggle against the commodity character of labour-power, that is, against capitalist production taken as a whole. The struggle against the fall in the relative wage is no longer a battle at the level of the mercantile economy but a revolutionary attack on the foundations of this economy; it is the socialist movement of the proletariat.[9]

The experiences gained during the militant [Italian] referendum campaigns for the recognition of 'common goods' need to be taken up, studied, and repeated under this banner.

Now, when it comes to the paradox of property, there seem to be no ways except those that end in confrontation and clash with the monetary and financial powers. If money is a means of account and exchange that is difficult to eliminate, it cannot be allowed to be an instrument of accumulation of power against the producers. How can one impose on the central bank the objectives of a production of humans for humans – that is, of bending to a biopolitical configuration of the social assets? The problem is not so much to separate deposit banks from investment banks, as it is to direct savings and investment towards balances that guarantee the production of humans for humans. This is a political battle to be waged immediately. It consists in rejecting the monetary governance* of biopower, this time without ideological reservations and without delay, that is, in introducing the possibility of a rupture and in giving it a democratic dimension. A 'currency of the common' is one that guarantees the reproduction and the amount of income that every citizen needs and the support for the forms of cooperation that constitute the multitude.

Let us now turn to the final paradox – the one between biocapital and workers' bodies. Here the contradiction cannot be overcome without eliminating one of the two poles; and, since capitalists cannot do without the worker, if they want to build profit, and the worker is never completely manipulable 'bare life' but is always living labour, the paradox will be overcome only by eliminating the capitalist.

Hence this is the proper terrain of politics, the terrain of deciding on the undecidable, with all its comings and goings, its pulling in and letting out, its killing and bringing to life, its fascism and democracy. So much on the side of power. But it is also the constituent terrain of all the machine-bodies, which are very peculiar, monstrous in their action. To these bodies, making politics means constituting the multitude institutionally, that is, plucking the singularities out of their solitude and setting them up in the *multitude*, or transforming the social experience of the multitude into a *political institution*. This transition materially takes the place of the idealistic operation that used to colour the concept of class consciousness. But it must also overcome the modern bourgeois – and twentieth-century – model of the relationship between constituent power and constituted power,[10] not because the constituent action fails, but because it can no longer be closed into the reconstruction of the 'One' of power. Uprisings are done not to seize power but to keep always open a process of

---

* 'governance' in English in the original.

counterpowers, challenging the ever new dispositifs of capture that the capitalist machine produces. It is on this ground that sovereign representation goes into crisis, because – drawn as it is into the mechanism of sovereignty and filtered through the sordid and magical alchemy of elections – it does not bear comparison with the truth and richness of the new social composition.

My impression is that, on the European constitutional front today, we need to build real buttresses against the neoliberal constitutions that they want to impose on us. We need to build a conflictual 'counter-democracy', which thrives on demands and protest, on resistance and anger. Away with normative constitutionalism: we need – and we build – biopolitical democracies, economic and material constitutions that do not live by turning into oppressive machines through the filter of legality and legal form but are run through investments of common money aimed at the continuous rebalancing of social relations; and these put the poor in the place of the rich and create a life shaped by humans in the service of humans.

And here it must be stated clearly, in the face of all the Nobel Prize winners in economics, that even growing productivity comes about only in an equal and happy society – a society of refusal of work.

But let us return to ourselves at this point. Let us try to understand what it means, in this new situation, to want to be property owners, and what it might be – for a worker, for each of us – to be an owner. All this, starting from a reality of work that takes place in the environment of interconnections and networks, services and subjectivations that I defined earlier. Here labour activity is immediately immersed into a network of cooperation. The labour of the individual can be valorized – but also realized simply on the market – only when it cooperates with other singularities that participate in the fabric of production. By way of generalization, we call this active community a 'multitude', in other words a set of cooperating singularities, and we note that the multitude becomes productive when such a condition of cooperation is realized.

Hence the observation that the constitution of the multitude in production takes place in a very complex way. In fact in this cooperation each singularity reappropriates for itself a specific portion of fixed capital, but this reappropriation can become productive only when it is immersed within the structure of social cooperation.

So what is this claim to a quantum of appropriation that the subject, once immersed in social production, can express? We recall a controversy of decades ago between Kelsen and Pašukanis,[11] when Kelsen, interpreting the latter, accused him of considering all law to be private law. Indeed, Pašukanis was still assuming that possessive individualism was the basis of the entire legal structure of society, starting from private law, and therefore in his view sovereignty was a projection of private property just as much as private property was a condition of sovereignty. But it is clear that, insofar as Pašukanis was living the political reality of a nascent socialism, these relations acquired in his eyes the urgency to find, in the labour of the individual citizen and through the demand for private property, the need for the common. As for us, when we express a desire for ownership, we have in mind the financial structures and the concept of private property as they stand today; all we do is express the need to be together, to produce together. And it is with this sense that we probably need to get back to Harrington and Winstanley.

When finance constitutes the totality of social labour – insofar as the latter is given as relational continuity in the time and space of a mobile, flexible and precarious labour – the request of ownership claims for labour a value that consists in its socialization.

It should be noted here that, in affirming this changeable relationship between labour and property in the formation of the concept of the common and in the establishment of an ontology of the common, I exclude any totalizing figure, any medievalizing nostalgia for property, be it private or public – but also common. It is labour that creates and modifies property. Therefore property cannot be given as a substantial concept any more, nor can the relationship between labour and property be fantasized as *Gemeinschaft* (just as, from this perspective, there is no place for concepts such as mass, people, nation, etc.).

So here the paradox of private property clashes with the reality of the common: a common that not only defines, like before, the dynamics of the forces of production, of the productive singularities immersed in the social relationship, but also represents that same process and renders it institutional from a monetary point of view. There is therefore, so to speak, a 'bad' ontology of the common that can manifest itself as a monetary function of property, as an anomic massification of labour, and as a populist identity of subjectivities; but there is also (and this begins to strengthen in people's awareness) a 'good' figure of the common, one that manifests itself as a desire for multitudinous cooperation among the singularities employed in the production process, of democratization from below of the activities of government, and of new constitutions of communal living.

It seems to me that the conclusions we have reached can be (easily) translated into those reached by Rodotà. We both believe, I would say, that the subject lays claim to the collective and to solidarity; and we both see the collective as being composed of singularities (not a mass or a flattening of differences, but a multitude or a composition of differences). If the common does not want to be organic, if it does not want to take on an identitarian essence, it needs to be desired as a way out of solitude, as a way to produce in cooperation and to exist in equality and solidarity. The right to have rights and to realize them takes root, and it has its source here.

In this respect I can return to the quotation from Marx with which I began, once again recognizing the power of its revolutionary intelligence. In fact I can say now that labour, transformed via labour, has become the foundation not of the affirmation of private property but of its abolition, and of having deprived it of the capacity to be a creative source of itself. The elimination of individualized and massified labour in favour of social and cooperative singularization entirely changes the reality of the organization of work. It will be my task to advance on this social terrain in order to bring to light the definitive emptying-out of the powers linked to private property.

Part III

Discussions

8
What Are We Willing to Share?

Reflections on a Concept of the Common in the Interregnum We Are Living*

Some time ago I was invited to a conference in which I was asked the question: 'What are we willing to share?' I was not able to attend the conference, but the question kept going round in my head. Here are some notes that I had written to open a discussion on the ethics of 'sharing' – a very fashionable topic today. Such is its fault – and yet it is a discussion that opens to further questions under the influence of technological development itself.

What are we willing to share? With a touch of irony we could say that this is a question that invites either reticence or hypocrisy. In today's realities, what can we share, what do we want to share, for instance with migrants? St Francis of Assisi offers us direct action, fraternal help or, better, giving (some of this resonates today in Pope Francis). And there is more. St Francis also claims that there is joy in giving, in giving oneself. The outcome? Everyone quotes him and is moved, yet nothing happens. But what happens if we take a secular position and say – without complacency but with a sense of responsibility – that we are willing to transfer a percentage of public welfare to refugees, or to help the poor here, *chez nous*, by offering communities of volunteers and some means of subsistence? In short, if we are willing to share – not very Christian, this – only the surplus? Is there a real sense of sharing in such behaviour? Or isn't this kind of sharing yet another opportunist and formal disposition? An initial response is required to these questions: under what conditions is it

---

* First published as 'Che cosa siamo disposti a condividere?' in Nikolai Blaumer, Johannes Ebert, Klaus-Dieter Lehmann and Andreas Ströhl, *Teilen und Tauschen*, Frankfurt: Fischer, 2017, pp. 290–310. The bracketed paragraphs are the author's later additions.

possible to share? Second, nowadays there is a lot of rhetoric around vulnerability and individual suffering. These are things that require care and sharing.* That may be so. But once you move out of the noise of box-ticking and neutralizing emotion, what does this mean? Care and sharing according to what criteria? For whom and in which direction? Put in these terms, the question again seems to be characterized by a high dose of insincerity. In my opinion the question becomes relevant only if it is put not in moral, individualistic terms but rather in ethical terms, which can claim some generality; if we interrogate not just benevolent singularities or minorities disposed towards emotional empathy and its derivatives, but a collectivity that is willing to *produce* through sharing; and if the question is addressed to the majority of men and women. The matter will then be one of sharing democratically, that is, according to the rule of negotiating the distribution of wealth – as when they made the Magna Carta; but in this case it would not be established between barons and city guilds but between the poachers and artisans of the 'forest'–suburb [*banlieu*] of Sherwood.†

But let's leave aside historical antecedents and turn to ourselves. I would like to proceed carefully, looking at earlier positions that have been expressed in this discussion. Max Weber makes a reasonable distinction, according to which any ethics-oriented activity can be brought under two divergent principles, in fact mutually incompatible; and this depends on whether the activity in question is oriented towards an ethics of responsibility or towards an ethics of conviction. Faced with this oppositional definition, classic and yet falsely neutral in the bourgeois world, I am rather in agreement with the bourgeois realism of good old Hegel, who thought of the transition from a morality of conviction (of love) to an ethics of responsibility not as a linear opposition but as a necessary gap in a logic that, by ascending to the universal, to the normative foundation, makes sure (in his view) that civil society itself exists and consists.

[As he illustrates the actions of the woman, the mother, the *mater familias* – agents of social actions (care, sharing) that he properly recognized as expressions of love – Hegel in fact adds a very characteristic argument in developing a suspension – *Aufhebung* – of the morality of conviction. The community creates its own subsistence

---

* 'care' and 'sharing' in English in the original, here and passim.
† Sherwood Forest in Nottinghamshire has historical associations with Robin Hood and royalty (here amalgamated with the urban notion of suburb).

only by destroying family bliss and by dissolving its own consciousness into that of a universal self. Along this road, it turns general femininity into an internal enemy, on account of what femininity represses (which is also essential to it). In the plot, this femininity – eternal irony of the community – alters the universal end of government by making it private and perverts the universal property of the state by making it a possession, a family ornament. And now that I have underlined the scandalous and infamous irrelevance with which women are evaluated in the metaphysics of the highest philosophical representative of the bourgeoisie, let us return to our argument: according to Hegel, sharing cannot but be regulated from above, which is where conviction and responsibility can be translated and based on historically validated and state-guaranteed norms and institutions. This 'Hegelian way' turned out to be fundamental much more than the 'Franciscan way' (or the 'Weberian way', that of responsibility), and was normalized in the praxis of modern bourgeois thought. But now that ethics has been invalidated in the crisis, or rather has been overwhelmed by a ferocious implosion after its nineteenth-century apogee. One could speak here of an 'irony of history' much more properly than Hegel did.]

It is then useful to show how much, in this critical implosion of modernity, sharing has lost its individual–relational characteristics and acquired rather relational–collective dimensions. Without overstating this transition, I should note that 'sharing' is now combined with 'production' when, in the transition from modernity to postmodernity, from the industrial to the post-industrial, the disciplinary (sharing) regime is replaced by sharing as a productive dispositif, according to which free subjectivities are prepared for collective production. In this they are controlled from above – when 'above' no longer means the authority of the state but the necessity of the market. Returning now to morality in this new situation, I wonder whether the problem should not be raised in a radically different way today by comparison with the good old days: we should perhaps recognize that those classic solutions falter – when they are not plainly invalidated by a new way of reasoning, according to common sense. And we should also appeal to new technological reasons. Actually the invitations to care and sharing seem to me to be – disguisedly, equivocally – symptoms that reveal this uncertainty. Moving beyond those older positions, I would now like to ask how it is possible to introduce a new ethical order when the rules of ancient morality are generally disregarded and, when it comes to sharing, every form of distributive justice (which those rules presuppose) has disintegrated. In fact we have to assume now the crisis of any definition of morality in the face of the current state of social life, in triumphant neoliberalism, and in the face of the decline of all traditional community loyalty. The market has won and ethics is subordinated to it. How is it possible to 'share', when any other act, being devoid of an ethical norm, has lost the capacity to be immediately referred to a responsible subject and is subjected to a heteronomous relationship, to a command that is often illogical, to a social ontology that is called 'market'? How is it possible to 'share', when the moral will that demands of us to conform to the norm and asks itself about its own value, therefore requiring an ethical foundation, fails to orient its intentionality? Doesn't the moral will itself dissolve? This is what happens today: insecurity and fear. Regimes of coexistence and affective regimes are immediately subjected to market rules; thus they become more and more alienated and alienating. If selfishness is preached as a virtue of the market, the transition from morality to ethics is, so to speak, blocked. Whatever the form of the norm – whether it's placed in the regime of conviction, in that of responsibility, or in that of state command (of biopower, we can say today, since we are convinced that Hegel's normative vulgate can be reduced, *mutatis mutandis*, to that concept) – in the face of a fragile and in any case heteronomous ethical perspective, then, all that remains is to take refuge in an individualistic morality of uncertain character. We are forced to behave with extreme selfishness, as if we had to face a condition of savage rarity – a condition in which one is allowed to let the other die in order to save oneself.

[This is the condition of acosmism, of passion against the other (as if the other did not constitute the cosmos) that Arendt denounces and posits as a possible base of all totalitarianism. In a beautiful book – *Un monde commun*[1] – Étienne Tassin sees this condition affirming itself in the multiple forms of violence that determine social exclusion. Balibar thinks that this same condition is capable of producing a tendential division between 'zones of life' (of a good life) and 'zones of death' (most often a dirty death).]

Thus we touch on the intolerability of the current condition. The question 'what are we willing to share?' has to be readdressed at this level. There is no point in complaining about its brutality. Sometimes – to qualify it – there is talk of a revival* of the state of nature. Always the same story! But this reference is crude and illusory, since brutality, violence and exclusion have now increased out of all proportion:

---

* 'revival' in English in the original.

they are given as part of the biopolitical fabric of a collective existence constructed by capitalist industry, and their effects are as profound and extensive as the capitalist invasion of *bios*. To put it differently: in relation to the state of nature, violence is incommensurable today, because here forms of life and production are built – and, especially, are perverted – that have already become collective and need to be ethically and politically recognized for what they are; but they are not and cannot be.

[Saskia Sassen protests against the ignorance of this condition in her *Expulsions*, after documenting the most terrible cases of 'expulsions' from homes, communities and nations, the violence of the North against the South and of the rich against the poor, the effects of technologies and the pathologies of financialization during the never-ending crisis that started in 2008. And she asks that all this be conceptualized, in other words no longer hidden – in short, that it be addressed as a problem in the social sciences. According to her, the spaces of those who have been expelled demand conceptual recognition. From a conceptual point of view, these spaces are underground sites that need to be brought back to the surface. But these are also, in principle, spaces full of potential for creating local economies, new stories, new ways of sharing.[2]]

Let's return to ourselves. The dissolution of morality as an individual determination of good and evil, according to a transcendental rule, and the emergence of an intractable egoism make it necessary not only to resist but, if possible, to restore a path between moral singularity and collective ethics. I think we can begin to do this by asking ourselves what is the collective today. Formally, the transition from an individualist morality to ethics implies in any case the construction of a *societas*, of a being together – whether weak or strong – and thus leads to the idea of a community, of a collective. It is this collective that is in question right now. The crisis of individualist morality and its weakened transfiguration into ethics have in reality thrown into doubt the very idea of collectivity.

In an attempt to deepen the critical perception of the collective, I would like first to reconsider the mode of production – the figure in which human beings produce their lives and means of survival. We know that today such a mode of production can be called biopolitical. In it, cognitive work, relational activities and productive cooperation have by now acquired clear prevalence over the forms of the old mode of production, where massified material labour was hegemonic. Those forms of command defined themselves through confrontation with that hegemony, by implanting themselves into that ontology. Now, conversely, the productive collective appears rather in multitudinous forms, as a set of singularities that communicate through networks and put their brains to work. They base themselves on a common productive substratum, on a commons* of knowledge and cooperation. To analyse processes of production today – bearing in mind that they are qualified in biopolitical terms – means becoming aware that it is not the massified individual who constitutes the productive collective, as was the case in industrialism, but the singularities in the network that recognize the collective, and recognize it as a common network rather than as a mass. Thus the 'collective' is founded on the 'common' – on a common that it continually produces and reproduces, a common that reveals itself in this way as the substantive foundation of the collective. And here it could be helpful to point out that, from 1968, this transformation began to be recognized in the development of (democratic) public opinion, too, and with increasing visibility after the rise of the movements in 2011. These are no longer masses or a collective hypostatized en masse; they are subjectivities that recognize that they are founded in communication, in the network, in making themselves common and that, by moving as just such subjectivities, build fields of social valorization and constituent political movements.

[Powers of cooperation constitute 'the sense of the social' [*le sens du social*], argues Franck Fischbach in a book of this title. And he urges us to go further and realize that in modernity work is more than the vector of the common (and not its gravedigger): it is the kind of entity that grants the common its specifically democratic form. Democratic capacity is inherent in work insofar as it essential to it – insofar as it is the political expression of this 'granting' property. This would be its cooperative dimension. Thus work is intrinsically political, and a politics intrinsic to work has an essentially democratic form.[3]]

A change in ethics certainly follows from this. Let us start by looking at it phenomenologically, without taking sides. We have been living for some time in a condition in which every moral problem unfolds socially. This, as we have seen, happens because the capitalist production of society and of life has become biopolitical, in other words has invested the social subjects, determining a totalization of domination that leaves no other space. We can recognize this production from the point of view of both power and the subjects. We know of course that in any case life, *bios*, is always marked by the dualism

---

* 'commons' in English in the original.

of commanding and resisting – even in the case of the real subsumption of society under capital. But let us not insist on this now. Let us consider rather that, on both these sides, there is a qualification of the collective that seems to have homogeneous aspects, at least at first sight. Whatever the point of view – capitalist or antagonist (working-class, social, etc.) – it seems clear that, in order to define the 'I', we must descend from the 'we', in other words that the social 'we' precedes the individual 'I'. To put it in the language of modern philosophy, in order to define itself, morality gets now displaced onto the terrain of ethics. In today's political and cultural crisis, in this interregnum that marks the transition between industrial and post-industrial and thus between various historical eras and civil cultures (a feature that should not be underestimated), we probably witness a breakdown of individual moralities (even if associative) in favour of new forms of 'making common'. In short, we witness a translation of sharing* (and distributive justice) into communing† (and participatory justice). As for the commutative justice of the markets, let's put it aside for now, because it is ungraspable in its financial incommensurability and seems capable of producing only social catastrophes. Beyond distributive justice, a participatory justice is therefore proposed, one articulated between singularity and communing. In this light, citizenship is communing, and this implies a radical new form of ethics.

[It is, however, tragic that the more the humanitarian reason [*la raison humanitaire*][4] develops and a new moral economy asserts itself in NGOs and in the voluntary sector, the more the ambiguity of all the forms of solidarity that exist in the capitalist world comes to the surface. Of course, as Fassin tells us, the tension between inequality and solidarity, between relations of domination and relations of assistance, is constitutive of all humanitarian governance, but the problem is not there; the problem is that the exchange is profoundly unequal. The people targeted – the subjects of this humanitarian attention – are well aware that they are expected to display the humility of the obligee rather than the stance of a person who has full rights.]

Second, let us return to multitudinous singularities and their mode of production via cooperation and cognitive power. This means returning to the antagonistic point of view in the biopolitical

---

* 'sharing' in English in the original.
† 'communing' in English on the original (here and in all subsequent occurrences in this chapter).

(capital) relationship, and therefore to the 'two' of the class struggle. It seems to me that, when the mode of production is considered in this light, it must be recognized that it shakes and can sow crisis at all the levels [*paliers*] of liberal civilization and capitalist structure of society – by which I mean private property and the market, corporate organizations and political representation. These institutions are closely linked: there is no market without private property and no political representation without multiple social coalitions of interest, corporations, parties, lobbying agencies and so on. Changing the combinations does not change the result. The crisis that these institutions are undergoing today is profound and chaotic. And if the transition to new forms of sociality, to communing, is given in an out-of-phase and dramatic manner, that is, within a long interregnum – if, as has already been said, the suffering of the individual and the non-suffering of the other, coupled with violence against oneself and the other, arise again in this unfinished transition, and the forces of implosion and exclusion become predominant – this means that the ethics of conviction, of responsibility or of authority, the ethics based on individualism, has not survived the transition. In this crisis, the desire for sharing and its spontaneous practices become confused and lose all sense of orientation. The moral propensity to move from the 'I' to reach the 'we' lacks a real foundation. That foundation resides only in the moral perception of a 'we'. We have to reverse the path of liberal individualism and to project its crisis onto a larger screen, looking at it as a deficiency of individualism in relation to the affirmation of the common.

The fact is that there are two ways of naming the collective and recognizing its ontology. Let us start from the simplest form of collective: the collective in production. Now, our cognitive experience and our moral question (at the extremes of that interregnum whose chaos we suffer but whose new diameter is known to us) mainly capture the form of the collective that is linked to industrialism. Why? Because in the crisis of industrialism and in the phenomena of globalization that are connected to it we can take into account the suffering and disorientation of that immense majority – the people who work in order to live and who suffer the command of capitalism and the huge and intolerable injustices of the global market. Well, the industrial collectivity has a history that begins with the completion of the primitive accumulation of capital, is confirmed in manufacturing, and develops along the entire period of big industry (we can use this useful Marxian terminology in describing this development). This story is therefore that of capitalist accumulation of surplus value and exploitation of a massified workforce. The mass: this is the fundamental characteristic, the essence of the collective as we knew it during the long age of industry. In this collective, individuals worked in proximity to other individuals, all being combined and put to work by objective powers, massified as equivalent agents of a task whose objectives were not set by them but that was commanded to them. It was a workforce that became a statistical whole, subsumed under capital. At the other pole of this critical arc I'm describing, at the level of that future to which the interregnum opens up, there is the multitudinous combination of singularities put to work. Here the productive collective is no longer a mass but a multitude. Here the one is not equivalent to the other but is singularly active. The one is defined by the other in an active relationship; the other by the others (each of whom is a singularity) in a common network in which they are composed and recomposed. Singularities (plural) and collective (singular) are mutually constructed: what can be seen here is a *common* collective. While in the massified collective the transition ran from the 'I' to the 'we', from individual morality to an abstract and repressive ethics, which crushes individuality into the flatness of equivalence, the multitudinous collective has nothing to do with arithmetic equivalence. It is a dynamic principle open to a concrete universality.

[This in no way means that this second figure of the collective is free from capitalist exploitation. In the so-called sharing economy, the collective use of goods does not seem to be able to change life. And in reality nothing changes. The common of Uber or Airbnb does not transform individual consumption into an economy of shared experiences, but renews individualistic egoism by multiplying it and further commercializes the time of sociality. So this means that exploitation can now be exercised in a manner that suits a new subject and a new form of productive association; that this subject will be characterized by a high autonomy, not collective but corporate; and, finally, that, for this reason, the violence of the capitalist relation becomes enormous and is perceived by the subject as intolerable.]

The radical difference that affects the concept and practices of sharing emerges with great clarity from this. In the massified collective, sharing is an exchange between individuals, a re-editing of the market, where individuals act according to interests (i.e. according to egotism). Here the sharing follows the opportunist characteristics that we have seen to create a crisis in individualist ethics. Here the 'I' acts as a prince, only to suffer the repercussions of a 'we' that is uncertain, if not unreachable. On the other hand, when we move to the terrain of the common collective, the possibility of building an ethics of sharing opens up to us. It is good, then, to recognize sharing in our existence and reciprocity in our being both products and producers of life. This well-being is continually rebuilt through our acting together; its value comes from our common production. Distributive justice no longer starts from the retracing of social stratifications (and from the quest for a balance among them); it is based on a common that produces and is produced by social development and that determines the conditions for participatory action. On this terrain, the distribution of goods is interpreted according to a schema of active and democratic equality.

[We should say that the word 'participation' should probably not be adopted here, because in the last decades it has been compromised in many utopian and mystifying experiences. Participation cannot be reduced, as has often happened, to a peripheral and subordinate addition to the administrative or productive machinery; it must be radical and ontologically constitutive from the perspective of the common. The collective is produced here as a political action of the 'we', in other words of 'doing together', of the construction and revelation of the common.]

In this context there are important experiences of sharing that take place in the digital arena. They are associated with activities such as Wikipedia or Free Software, for example, but can also be observed in other recent areas, which see experiences of sharing specialized knowledge, of producing money and cooperation in banking, and so on in addition to sharing cars, apartments and suchlike. Particularly interesting is the project of (productive) sharing cooperatives proposed by Trebor Scholz. Alongside those sophisticated activities, there are millions of cooperative sharing experiences that range from the cultivation of marijuana in social centres to the rebuilding of companies that have fallen into bankruptcy and are left out of the market. This is the realm of 'minorities' – what Guattari and Deleuze indicated as a 'place of ethicity'. The problem is obviously one of transforming these places of minor surplus into major surpluses of productive and political power [*potenza*].

As we have seen, from the division between forms of the collective that has been drawn here it does not follow that the second model of collective can be represented as a subject removed from exploitation or, more generally, that it can be given as an autonomous power, free of the negative. Too often, however, dominant opinion reacts to any forefronting of open possibilities, of pulsating virtualities, of trends in the making by caricaturing these claims as miraculous and by asking for their 'realistic' (sic!) reduction (in no way caricatural). This is neither more nor less than an attempt to suppress those powers of the real, as if they were reduced and marginal forms of experience, and to confirm the insurmountable consistency and insurmountable form of the exploitation of every collective at work. Well, leaving aside those insulting reductions, I, too, refused to grant here, deceptively, an autonomous consistency to the cooperative collective that emerges in the new mode of production, or to establish the independence of these subjectivities. No: this new collective, too, exists in a historical situation that is characterized by the totalization of capitalist command. It therefore undergoes the latter's determinations. But at the same time we have to say that, while a certain homogeneity emerges between the two types of collective in the current historical cycle – in the interregnum, in the temporal tension in which they are placed – there exist nevertheless virtualities of rupture of all convergence and of departures in the directions of development. So each time the power relationship (concretized in command over production) is modified – in the struggles that constantly traverse the capital relation – the dual consistency of the collective (which is currently subordinated but virtually reactive) could either be transformed by and incorporated into the violent mutation of capital (and the tendential autonomy of cooperation could be consequently destroyed) or be qualified by the social struggles of class liberation each time the power relationship goes in the opposite direction – and this would determine the cancellation of the massified model of cooperation and of the domination of capitalist exploitation. These conditions of rupture have exploded and these powers of the 'second', the 'other', the 'double power' – that of the class struggle – have been historically realized at other times in the development of capitalist accumulation, in other cases of exploitation and in other figures of resistance. This is what happened in the initial phases of the great revolutions of the Short Century.

[In the succession of struggles against the post-2011 crises, at the height of that condition of interregnum that we were living through, the transition to communing has manifested itself very powerfully. From many quarters there came a call to reread distributive justice as participatory justice, or rather to attribute to the constitutive dynamics of distributive justice a dispositif that might recompose the singularity and the common. Here the anthropological and ethnographic exploration of the indigenous common has played an important role. The concept of living well [*buen vivir*] – when we remove it from the alienating publicity that has invested it and bring it back to the heart of indigenous cultural experiences, when we liberate it from the form of a welfare for indigenous people (and thus from being subjected to the misery of financial regulation) – seems very much to represent one of the faces of communing.]

But, when framed this way, our argument still seems to configure a utopian horizon – even when 'utopia' designates a rational dispositif that, traversing the real, opens to the future – rather than a material index of new ethical behaviours. So let us now return to ourselves, to the questions I asked at the beginning of this lecture. What, then, are we willing to share? Bearing in mind the elements we know outlined here, this is clearly a question of 'sharing life'. So let us ask ourselves once more the core question: what does sharing mean, when it comes to refugees? What does sharing mean in the face of the enormous increase in the precariat, in its poverty and in its powerless power? What is required today is not an act of conviction (or love) or of Weberian responsibility; rather we need to go beyond these two forms of ethics of associated life, denouncing their ineffectiveness and hypocrisy. We cannot continue to play off abstract terminological opposites and mystify the choice in a game that necessarily ends up being opportunist. Here sharing means recognizing everybody's right to life – not out of love or as an act of responsibility, and not because we are commanded to do so, but simply because life, along with producing, is a common thing. The right of refugees to cross borders and become citizens and that of precarious workers to become workers is established within this common. Any other choice, whether made out of conviction or responsibility, out of love or reason, is a choice that amounts to 'not letting live'; and this can end up in 'making people die'. It is within these dimensions that the theme of sharing needs to be addressed today.

It is reasonable to recognize that sharing life with others and putting it in common is the only basis on which one can live an ethical life. But this recognition is also tragic because, while making people die has become trivial, living together and sharing without market and hypocrisy – in short, realizing the common – is too often viewed as irresponsible and not the thing to do, a 'bad thing', if not actually a crime. In this situation it is right and urgent to rebel!

9
The Metaphysics of the Common*

Present Times

The new book by Pierre Dardot and Christian Laval deals with the theme of 'the common'. It details meticulously the theoretical paths that have characterized the topic. But it limits reflection to a terrain where there is no room for a critique of the real forms of exploitation and private expropriation of collectively produced wealth.

After *Marx, prénom Karl*,[†] Dardot and Laval offer us a 'Proudhon, prénom Pierre-Joseph'. In Italy such a title would be enough to guarantee the book's failure; it would recall the reactionary operation carried out in the 1970s by Pellicani and Coen (among others) in *Mondo Operaio*, under the inspiration of Craxi. But this book is certainly not like that. It introduces the debate on the common in France, and hopefully reopens it in Europe. So let's turn to the book. While the book on Marx was characterized by a resolute deteleologization of socialism (I mean, a reasoned critique of any socialist theory that wanted to encapsulate the final project and force of communist liberation within capitalist development), this second book[‡] is characterized by a resolute dematerialization of the concept of socialism. Such is the operation developed in this 'essay on revolution': it is a real liquidation of historical materialism, of the Marxist

---

* First published as 'La metafisica del comune', *Il Manifesto*, 6 May 2014, p. 8.
† Pierre Dardot and Christian Laval, *Marx, prénom Karl*, Paris: Gallimard, 2012.
‡ Pierre Dardot and Christian Laval, *On Revolution in the 21st Century*, London: Bloomsbury, 2019.

critique of the political economy of mature capitalism, in the name of a new 'principle'. *Common*: not 'commons', not 'the' common, but 'common', as a principle that animates both the collective activity of individuals in the construction of wealth and life and the self-government of these activities.

To achieve such liquidation, a precise framework of ideas is presented and discussed. The point of departure is the priority of the common as a principle of transformation of the social. This priority is asserted before establishing the opposition of a new right of use to the right of property. Next, the authors state that the common is the principle of liberation of work and that common enterprise and association must prevail in the sphere of the economy. They also talk about the need to re-establish social democracy, the need to transform public services into an 'institution' of the common and the need to form or 'invent' a 'global federation of commons worldwide'.

An idealistic vision

This political clarification of the principle of the common is preceded by a long work of critical and constructive analysis that develops in two stages. The first stage, 'The Emergence of the Common', reconstructs the historical context that has seen the affirmation of the new principle of the common and critiques the limits of conceptions offered in recent years by economists, philosophers and jurists as well as by activists. The second part, 'Law and the Institution of the Common', seeks to re-establish the concept of the common more directly by placing it on the terrain of law and institution. The book, which is the outcome of the seminar 'Du public au commun' (amply and contradictorily developed at the Collège international de philosophie from 2011 to 2013), deepens the idea of the common mainly by reference to the current of associationist socialism, which goes back from Proudhon to Jean Jaurès and Maxim Leroy, then forward to Mauss and Gurvitch, and finally to the late Castoriadis of *The Imaginary Institution of Society*, without ever escaping the attempt to absorb some traits of Marxian thought into this 'idealistic' development of the project of a future socialism. The effect produced by the critique and reconstruction of the concept of the common, as canvassed in this book, is unavoidably idealistic because, continuing the theme of Proudhon against Marx, the correct and increasingly effective break with any telos of socialism is followed by a no less obsessive *dematerialization* of the concept of capital and of the context of the class struggle – so that by the end of the book it is no longer clear how the common is to be claimed, where the subjects who build it are to be found, or what figures in the development of capital constitute its background.

An icy wind blows across this idealist scenario – a strong pessimism, almost a resigned realization that the production of subjectivity *on the capitalist side* is materially implacable and historically irresistible. Before us lie the subjugation of the workers and the internalization of command, which is increasingly harsh in the age of cognitive capital – as the current science of management[*] would have it and as the new suffering experienced by the workers themselves bears witness (with the aid of labour psychology). So how can we define the 'common'? As a community of shared suffering? Or a god who has to save us?

In my view, in order to re-establish the concept of the common, we should begin by following a path similar to that followed by Dardot and Laval. The critique they offer of the notion of 'common' in its theological, juridical and ecological figures – in sum, in all its forms of objectification or reification, which tirelessly repeat themselves in this respect – and also of the philosophical notion, which tends to trivialize the 'common' into a 'universal', is correct. A true concept of 'common' can be arrived at only through a conscious political praxis and must therefore consist of an *instituting* process [*processo* istituente], of a dispositif of institutions of the common. The common has its origin not in objects or metaphysical conditions but only in activity.

Beyond the tragedy of the commons

In this context, Dardot and Laval's critique of Elinor Ostrom's ecology of the commons[†] is undoubtedly masterful, because it clarifies the liberal and individualistic nature of that ecology: a system of norms is set in order to deal with the 'tragedy of the commons', in other words to safeguard the accessibility and preservation of the commons on the capitalist side, as 'natural assets'. But if one follows the path indicated by Dardot and Laval, one soon reaches a junction, which opens up when one realizes that the common is not simply the product of generic (anthropological and sociological) activity but

---

[*] 'management' in English in the original.
[†] 'commons' in English in the original (here and next).

the outcome of *productive activity*. Here the confrontation with Marx becomes inevitable and decisive.

And yet Dardot and Laval seem overwhelmed by the complexity of the question. On the one hand, their radically desubstantializing (idealist?) hypothesis of the common pushes them to underestimate the same 'social' dimension of the common as the one proposed by Proudhon; on the other hand, it makes them accuse the Marxists who have tackled the theme of the common (taking into account the new 'social' nature of exploitation) of being 'unconsciously' Proudhonists. Let us examine a few points that might take us beyond this confusion. It is obvious to all (and undoubtedly also to Dardot and Laval) that capitalist development has reached a level of 'abstraction' (in the Marxian sense of the definition of value) and therefore a capacity for exploitation that extends over the whole of society. Within this dimension of exploitation a sort of perverse common is being built: that of an exploitation that is exercised over and against the whole of society, over the whole of life. Capital has become a global biopower. To Dardot and Laval, awareness of this global reach and invasiveness of biopower, or rather of the power of the perverse common, recalls the arguments of the critique of teleology denounced in Marxist socialism, as if the fact of biopower constituted a new teleological drift. But can the correct underlining of Marxian limits to the dialectical analysis of capitalist development perhaps erase *the current dimensions of capitalist biopower*, or perhaps make us forget them?

Dardot and Laval's critique of David Harvey's exploitation by dispossession and of all the neo-Marxist analyses that have glimpsed, in the Marxian model of original accumulation, analogies with what happens now at the global level – namely an extractive exploitation – is equivocal because it denies the problem while criticizing its solution. And all the more as this critique totally ignores the function of finance capital (or the productive function of money, interest and rent) when it accuses other Marxist authors – authors concerned with the recomposition of rent as an instrument of exploitation and as a new figure of profit – of having reduced profit, à la Proudhon, to the 'theft' of a substantialized, common 'thing'.

A theft of surplus labour

Here, in developing their critique, Dardot and Laval seem to forget the most basic features of Marxian thought – especially that capital is not an independent essence, a Leviathan, but a *production-based relationship of exploitation* and that, in the current condition, financial capital invests a world of production that is socially organized, accumulating in the extractions of surplus value both the direct exploitation of working-class labour along with the expropriation of natural assets, territories and structures of the welfare state, and the indirect extraction of social surplus value through the exercise of monetary domination. If you want to call all this 'theft', I would not be scandalized: using this word doesn't make you a Proudhonist, as long as you give it the meaning that capital gives it today, namely a mode of accumulation directly grafted onto the new forms of the labour process and its socialization – both in the individual dimension and in its associative figure. When Marx says that the capitalist appropriates the excess of value that cooperation between two or more workers brings about, he certainly does not deny that at the same time capital has also appropriated the surplus labour of individual workers. Here 'theft' includes the exploitation of surplus labour and renders capital even more indecent than it has always been in developing production.

In Dardot and Laval's *Marx* one sensed a touch of Foucault (I mean, of a historical approach that pays attention to agent subjectivities). But now this streak has faded away – and in doing so it has also removed the fruit, which was a lively and dynamic look at the history of capitalism. Here, in the absence of a historically reflexive methodology, lies beyond doubt a Durkheimian – perhaps even categorial and Kantian – approach to capitalist development. Capital appears to be a timeless and all-powerful machine. Real subsumption is not seen as the conclusion of a historical process but only as a figure in the process of enlarged reproduction of capital.

Without class and capital

Alongside this, however, a certain historicity is reintroduced when the two authors discuss, in a historically extensive manner, the destructive and ever more real efficacy of the capitalist production of, and on, the subjectivities at work. *Class struggle would no longer exist.* This seems to be the final hypothesis in a conception that began by excluding the class struggle – understood in Marx's sense – from the constitution of the concept of capital. It appears that the dematerialization of the common, so heavy-handedly carried out, and the exclusive definition of the common as 'action', as a principle of activity, correspondingly imply the dematerialization of the class struggle, as if even the excessive insistence on a capitalist production of labour subjectivities internally subjected to command implied the negation of productive subjectivity as such.

But without productive subjectivity there is not even a concept of capital. So, in the end, in the face of the historical change of exploitation (which is here misunderstood), in the face of capital's being defined more and more as 'social power' (which is here denied), in the face of such an extensive emergence of the common, imposed by the creation of a new *mode of production* (and it should be noted that this emergence has already brought about new forms of *labour process*) – in the face of all this we forget that only living labour is productive, that only subjectivity is resistant, that cooperation alone is powerful, and that, in consequence, the common is not simply 'activity', but an activity that produces wealth and life and transforms labour. The *common* is not an ideal (although it may be that, too) but it is the very form in which the *class struggle* is defined today. I have a question for Dardot and Laval: if today the common is not a desire implanted in the critique of productive activity, and if it shines only before our consciousness numbed by the violent penetration of biopower, if it is simply a 'principle' – what is there that incites us to struggle? Dardot and Laval seem to reply that the principle of the common is a category of activity, of the institution – it is not based on the real but founds the real – it cannot be conquered but eventually you administer it (they argue for this at length, and the concept will be taken up elsewhere). So why struggle?

But, beyond any criticism, this is a book that reopens the debate on the common, and no one will be surprised that it has also reopened the debate on communism.

May 2014

10

The Revolution Will Not Be an Explosion Somewhere down the Road

An Interview with Antonio Negri*

Filippo Del Lucchese and Jason E. Smith

FILLIPPO DEL LUCCHESE AND JASON E. SMITH For some years now, your most important works have been written with Michael Hardt, and his contribution has become increasingly clear, especially in your most recent book, *Commonwealth*.[1] This evolution is even more evident for those who know your prior work, marked as it is by a thought and a form of writing that are highly original and by a style that emerges through your political and cultural experiences.

How do you work together, and what are the most important elements that result from this encounter?

ANTONIO NEGRI Our way of working is well known. We have long discussions, and we develop schemas together, after which the work is divided up. After having written our respective parts, we revise them together. The final version is written in Italian or in English and translated as we proceed. The mechanism therefore involves a continuous 'collusion' of arguments and manners of expression.

Being the oldest, I am probably the one who was most involved in the beginning. But the process has become increasingly equal between us. There is no doubt that a certain argumentative style – rather American – is typical of Michael and his character. He does not like, for example, polemics that are too forceful. I believe there is a real effort, and not only in terms of language, to respect certain

---

* First published in *Grey Room*, 41 (2010): 6–23, under the same title.

forms of academic writing. In any case, it is always through discussion and debate that we arrive at the precise form our theses will take. This is a significant change from my earlier books. My form of writing was more directly linked to political confrontation. But, above all, it was more solitary: after all, many of my earlier books were written in prison.

FDL/JES At the same time, a large part of the elaboration of your theses is due to the concrete experience of the struggles of recent years.

'The intellectual', you write in *Commonwealth*, 'is and can only be a militant, engaged as a singularity among others, embarked on the project of co-research aimed at making the multitude' (p. 118).

In what way does the accumulation of struggles and experience enter into your work?

AN The relation to these struggles is undoubtedly not as close as it was for me in the past, above all in the 1970s. And our relation is more balanced, less tied to the immediate adherence to certain interpretative paradigms or certain slogans. As often happens in militant situations, you have to be harder, less refined. Above all, there is no doubt that an accumulation of experiences is at the foundation of our discourse. This osmosis is more closely tied to this accumulation than to the immediacy of the political relation. Some time ago, I had a debate with some comrades about the last pages of Foucault's final course, on cynics and militant thought.[2] These are remarkable pages, but I find that I've moved away from them a little at this point… maybe because of age. These are pages I no longer read in ethical terms. I insist more emphatically on the extraordinary theoretical elements they contain.

FDL/JES Is it possible to invert Althusser's beautiful phrase – calling himself a 'political agitator in philosophy' – in speaking of your role as an intellectual, defining yourself instead as a 'philosophical agitator in politics'?

AN Yes, but precisely in its inverted form. Althusser was a teacher and a friend, but his attempt to be the 'political' in philosophy always bothered me. I am convinced, as he said, that philosophy is a *Kampfplatz*, a battlefield where theoretical positions clash.[3] And yet with him there was always the excessive abstraction of the 'professor' or of the subject who engages in politics in and through philosophy, and that I do not share. The fact that, ultimately, for him both philosophical language and the history of philosophy are posited as theoretical references also bothers me. To be a philosopher in militancy reverses this perspective, allowing you to take on the problem concretely rather than abstractly. This is where the difference between a philosophy solidly planted in the biosphere, real life, and an abstract philosophical sphere becomes clear. And this is also the case from the point of view of language as well as of the ends, tactics, and way problems are confronted and addressed.

FDL/JES   In *Commonwealth* we find a reactivation of two terms – the common and commonwealth – which evoke, to an Anglophone ear, the period of the English Civil War and the messianic communism of the Levellers and Diggers. Why is it important to reactivate these two concepts? Are we, as has been proposed by Paolo Virno, entering a new seventeenth century?[4]

AN   In all probability, yes. This means – it's an idea that I always had in mind (at least when I published *Political Descartes* in 1975)[5] – that the crisis of the Renaissance has analogies with the phase of the crisis of modernity we live in; that the crisis of the modern corresponds to this current phase of the invention of... what should it be called?... of communism. Actually it's better to speak of the age of the postmodern, or of the 'common' – because the new form of accumulation of capital currently functioning repeats for the first time the processes of expropriation of the common typical of the beginnings of modernity. It's a process that attacks life and the common that the century of worker struggles before us built: the 'commons' that have become the basis of our existence, from welfare to the new capacities to produce, act and build common languages other than the technoscientific. Resistance acts against this new accumulation, and this is the central point of *Commonwealth*. We call it 'the one divides into two', indicating a bifurcation that resistance builds in the present. An absolutely central bifurcation, then, which is founded on the defence of the common and the attempt to valorize, against the new primitive accumulation, the value of the commons.

Can this be represented in eschatological terms, as it was during the English Revolution? Unlikely. Every eschatology refers to an 'outside', whereas the elements of destruction appearing today, the coming apocalypse, are totally internal. There is no more transcendence. We move on a plane of complete immanence. Consequently, the apocalyptic or eschatological elements showing up today – various conceptions of radical evil, for example – can only be a weapon in the hands of the enemy. The first element is therefore the perception of a rupture, or of a bifurcation that today appears within capitalist development: the matter used within the production process today is, in fact, a matter that is not consumed or used up. It's intelligence. Its liberatory force, the force deployed in the defense of the common and in a construction starting from the common, is virtually irresistible. And if virtuality is not actual, it represents all the same a possibility. There is always resistance.

FDL/JES Let's stick with this liberation, while remaining at the conceptual level. One of the more intriguing arguments you make in *Commonwealth* is that the idea of communism must be completely divorced from the 'illusions' of socialism, understood as a form of public management of production and as a disciplinary regime of work. You found this distinction on the asymmetry between the 'public' and the 'common': 'what the private is to capitalism and what the public is to socialism, the common is to communism' (p. 273). Can you elaborate on this distinction between the public and the common? What does it mean to be a communist today?

AN To be a communist means to struggle against private property and ultimately destroy it, and to build the institutions of the common. However, this means also and equally thinking that it is no longer concretely possible to develop production and thus create the collective without freedom and equality – abstract universals – being integrated into the heart of the process of the common, of the concrete, historical institution and constitution of the collective. These universals should become concrete or, better, common. Multitude, communism: it's the idea of a collective, but of a collective as an articulation of singularities. To be communist means, consequently, building forms of 'norming' the real that are dynamic, political constitutions that modify themselves in view of the continuous modifications of the production and reproduction of the multitude. It's a 'making the constitution' around the necessity of a common production, accompanied by the need to conquer happiness.

Russian historical communism (maybe Chinese communism) was – this is its good side – a socialism, a public management of the production of wealth. It was defeated, but it offered us the image of a real possibility. I believe this sentiment courses through the whole book. It is not the utopian sentiment of an ideal possibility. To the contrary, it is the consciousness of a *Faktum* that cannot be defeated or undone, of a reality that cannot be refuted, of an irreversible process. *The Future Has an Ancient Heart* was the title of a novel by Carlo Levi (an apologia for the Soviet Union).[6] It's a phrase I have always heard with a great deal of irony – and I still do – but in which there is, at bottom, something true.

FDL/JES   If we no longer consider the project of 'building socialism' as an intermediate phase between the capitalist mode of production and the collective appropriation of the common, how are we to reconceptualize the idea of transition? Is it possible to pass directly from the biopolitical production of contemporary capitalism to communism in the sense you understand it?

AN   We no longer have any need whatsoever for a transition. What counts today is the bifurcation. This means that we already live through a radical and profound transformation, but it also indicates something fundamentally different from the idea of transition such as it has been theorized in preceding socialist experiences. The current movement is not a transition from one mode of production to another but the construction of the other, the development of the alternative from now on visible from within our history, clarified through antagonism.

This perception leads to another fundamental node, more methodological than metaphysical: the refusal of the dialectic.

When we speak of bifurcation in Deleuzian or Foucauldian terms, we speak of the construction of a dispositif that detaches itself from the determined historical course because it produces subjectivity. (It would certainly be possible, at the limit, to repropose, from within this detachment, a certain dialectic: the relation tactics–strategy, for example, often implies dialectical elements.) However, the origin of this detachment, of this movement of bifurcation, is not oriented towards a totality or a new global subsumption or an *Aufhebung*.* What we have here is a difference, which affirms itself, and is exalted, in a dispositif, a path, a trajectory, in which institutional elements are born. It is not the institutionalization of civil society that Hegel exalts and that anarchists detest. It is also not the traditional concept of institution that drags along with it theologico-political characteristics. It is not a necessity but a construction. And what's more, it possesses the capacity to continually renew itself.

Bifurcation demands an institution. This is how the new is built through a 'common' accumulation that gives a sense to the world that today surrounds us. To desires, to work. We have torn them away from capital. Simply think of the quantity of fixed capital we carry within us. Some time ago I had a discussion with some comrades who said, like Karl Heinz Roth, that fixed capital is something

---

* Abolition, annulment.

suitable only for a slave.[7] The slave is a fixed capital, they argue, not the contemporary, cognitive, intelligent, mobile worker... It's not true! There is another fixed capital, one we are not, like the slave, a mere projection of – a fixed capital that we have reappropriated, that we have turned inside out, into our capacity for mobility and intelligence. Even while we are enslaved by capital, we are rebellious, we flee. To be mobile, intelligent, to possess languages, to be capable of freedom – these are not natural givens. It is a power, a potentiality, the product of a creative resistance.

FDL/JES Let's speak about the horizons and possibilities of struggle in the era of biopolitical production. You start from analyses of *operaismo* that underline the priority and anteriority of worker struggles over capitalist development – and therefore from struggles as the motor of development and restructuration of capital, always compelled to respond to worker offensives. This priority and anteriority is even more visible today in the conditions of biopolitical production, where 'one divides into two' and the multiple and plural subjectivity of the multitude – as productive – separates and definitively flees a management that has become sterile and parasitic.

In this context, how and against what, concretely, is it possible to rebel? In prior struggles we had the revolt against work, against the time of work, which was exploited, in view of raising wages and increasing free time. Today how is it possible to refuse work, if work coincides with life? How is it possible to 'sabotage' work without renouncing one's own essence? How can we destroy work without destroying society, or destroy the time of work without destroying free time?

AN I recently read a book by Daniel Cohen, who today is among the best-known economists in France (when he was younger, I dedicated *Marx beyond Marx* to him, as well to some others).[8] Cohen argues that the new anthropological figure of the worker, the ideal type of the worker, after this crisis, is the intellectual–cognitive worker, and that the elements of community are built around these elements. The cognitive and the mobile are therefore the two cardinal points of the contemporary anthropology of the worker: the productive, mobile point of a multitudinous intersection. Production – and the political constitutions that emerge from it – would therefore have to be imagined on this basis. From this point of view (within projects of resistance and constitutive power), the refusal of work, today still, is (as it was, in the same way, for the Fordist worker) and will be a determined refusal. No one has ever spoken of an absolute refusal of work. If we take the most beautiful documents on the refusal of work, for example those of the Marghera petrochemical workers in the 1970s – in the journal *Lavoro zero* (*Zero Work*), for example – we see that it was a completely determined refusal, through which it was possible to contest working hours, wages, the subjection of free time, rents and so on. It's the same thing today: the refusal of work is an absolutely determined refusal.

Over the past few days I participated in an investigation into recent suicides in large French firms. It turns out that what the employees were refusing was a determined way of organizing work. Their stories speak of new conditions of work in gigantic 'open spaces': the workers are confined to the circumscribed space of their cubicle, facing their computers. In a total fragmentation of the production process, the worker is forced to invent while not knowing where his cognitive activity is going. No consciousness of the ensemble of the production process is permitted. And the fragmentation is then accentuated, clashing with marketing processes that are separate from and in contradiction with the production process. All this is bathed in a noisy hum not unlike that found in the old Fordist factory. This is the theatre of a multiplication of alienation and emergence of madness that the worker is forced to drag along with her, in her life outside the firm. And vice versa, for the cognitive worker, everything that happens in her life outside the firm immediately lands on her work desk, as a new source of alienation and worry, to the point where a family tragedy, a boss's heavy-handedness, or simply a lack of career success provokes suicide. This is the terrain to which we should bring the refusal of work, in the sense of a determined refusal of these work conditions.

In addition to all this, what makes work still more unbearable is the fact that we have a capacity to develop a high productivity and to build new worlds: vital productivity, the capacity to apply desire to matters of life. It is in this contradiction that struggles should today be invented. Indeed, struggles don't just spring up out of nowhere. They go slowly and are progressively built, with difficulty, starting from determined contradictions. Built, organized, as happened in the time of Fordism: strikes were never spontaneous but always constructed, progressively, around a combination of wage objectives and the protests of life against work. You can have an excellent objective, but if you do not succeed in cohering around the life of workers, the objective and the struggle fail.

The same thing goes today. But how to organize this new subject?

How is the new form of exploitation perceived by the cognitive workers of large firms? Everyone immediately says that the traditional unions are no longer useful for anything. In the first place because it is necessary to operate on an international and global plane, and the unions have not managed to do this yet. And then because the unions have not been able to grasp the complexity of the vital whole that is at the root of these struggles. The unions concern themselves with employment, and are in this sense corporate (and thus precisely not political: this is where the disaster lies). It is necessary therefore to indicate new, alternative forms of organization. What can we do to organize this intelligent raw material and make it bifurcate, bringing it outside the direction of capital?

This is where new forms of mutualism and propositions for alternative organizations of work emerge, as well as for alternatives to the wage system. These are not Proudhonian discourses! These are proposals for organizing cooperatives and other mutualist forms that directly attack the financial levels of the organization of work. Struggles that are not doomed to defeat can be organized only at this level. We are moving through a phase in the cycle of worker struggles that has demonstrated the exhaustion of the old forms and that stakes a claim for a different strategic intelligence: the intelligence to interconnect struggles from various and diverse fronts. They can come from ecology, the factory, social work, services and so on. It is, in sum, a matter of reuniting all the sectors in which the new conditions of production are developing. The discourse we hold in our book on the intersection of struggles is, from this point of view, fundamental. I do not believe that today there is any possibility of seizing a central point on the horizon of struggles: only their intersection has a strategic significance.

FDL/JES For you, the institution of happiness is not only a political process; it is an ontological one as well. It is on this point that you propose, in a strong philosophical gesture, to bring together materialism and teleology or, better, to formulate a materialist teleology that would nevertheless entail no ultimate ends that would guide this process (p. 378).

How does this process dodge the risk of thinking the encounter among singularities in and by the multitude not as aleatory, as Machiavelli, Spinoza, and then later Althusser do, but as necessary and teleologically guided? It sometimes seems that the 'advent' of the multitude as subject of the common is only a question of time, or that it is already given, or that the fact that it has not happened is an exception and not the rule.

AN The problem of the relation between teleology and materialism is a little like that of the chicken and the egg: easy to verify and hard to explain. It is clear there was a phase during which a large part of contemporary critique was unleashed against teleology (particularly ferocious with regard to the critique of communism and of the golden future the Soviet revolution was to have brought about), considering it to be the philosophical figure of an opportunist, instrumentalist finalism that was increasingly discredited. Then, little by little, the discourse against teleology became a discourse against materialism. Now the discourses have been taken back up and clarified. As far as I am concerned, there is no need to worry about dialectical materialism, the famous diamat. Historical materialism is something else entirely. In historical materialism, the finality of action is bound in no deterministic way to the success of its realization. That would be Hegelianism. The relation between act and end is always aleatory in historical materialism. We remove from the idea of telos every sense of necessity. But this does not mean that we remove the telos from action. The subjectivity–singularity must, therefore, now take it on. That said, why not seize the possibility of constructing a universality through common action? That this universality might entail ambiguous elements and drift towards the irrational is obvious enough. It is nevertheless possible that this universality can be implemented in a process of common construction. I think that it is the process of constructing common notions and common institutional wills, as is witnessed in other experiences of materialist thought. On this point, the aleatory is not excluded but is rather proposed for open discussion, in a confrontation between diverse finalities, on the basis of which we can claim that a communist institutionalization or the force of the common – which becomes increasingly fundamental – can triumph. In conclusion, there is no 'advent' of the multitude, and still less of communism. All we do is aleatory. But construction is always possible. We express the desire of the common, and no one can stop us from doing so.

FDL/JES On many occasions, in the latter part of *Commonwealth* you claim a fidelity to the great tradition of anthropological realism of Machiavelli and Spinoza, among others (p. 185). These are philosophers not of resignation and pessimism, but of polemical realism, of the theory of indignation, of conflict as the essence of the multitude. On other occasions, however, you speak of the necessity of a transformation of the human to come (p. 378), of the creation of a new humanity (pp. 118, 361), of the construction of a new world (p. 371). With these terms you claim to be developing Foucault's assertion *l'homme produit l'homme*, that is, 'what ought to be produced is not man as nature supposedly designed it, or as his essence ordains him to be – we need to produce something that doesn't yet exist, without being able to know what it will be'.[9] A concept, therefore, that is profoundly foreign to the realist tradition and that cannot be found in the pages of Machiavelli and Spinoza.

Is it a question, on this point, of going 'beyond' these authors?

How do you redefine anthropological realism?

AN We have been impressed by some of the work done in Latin America; for example, that of Viveiros de Castro, who is a great figure of anthropology coming in the wake of the structuralism of Lévi Strauss. The biopolitical context of anthropological mutations is here completely restored, with a great deal of insistence on the productivity of living in common. On the other hand, we have always held, on a Marxist terrain, that the technopolitical modification of the current form of capital would determine modifications that would affect not only the form of work but the subjects of work as well. The passage from the peasant to the non-skilled worker, then from the skilled worker to the worker of the large company, and so on, all of that relates to the anthropological plane. It is still more evident today, in the era of globalization. It concerns a modification (probably a veritable metamorphosis) that we have not yet managed to define fully but that obviously cuts across this new composition of work, this multitude that works and the singularities of which it is composed.

I mentioned this report by Daniel Cohen that really struck me: the relation between the cognitive and mobility as the fundamental characteristic of the new way of producing, as the deepening of the intersection of work in the webs of information, which intensifies to the point that a new mode of production is configured – whence the figure of a new worker subject, actor of the emergence of subjectivity in the productive context: a characteristic profoundly different from that of the typical worker of our and our fathers' generation. It is this revolutionary anthropological modification that should be studied. Languages themselves now constitute a bias, and this presents itself as event and as institution. The present work is an attempt to redefine the materiality of the transformations occurring now, to understand the common as something invented, as something that institutes itself. We can say that here we have a passage 'from quantity to quality', indicating not only the intensity of the leap that we are witnessing, the force of the constituent power that becomes constituted, but just as much the ontological hardness of this event, a new *Wirklichkeit* (reality). It is therefore important to avoid Badiou's abstraction, which constructs an enormous machine in order to take away all ontological consistency from the event!

FDL/JES   In the 1960s we spoke of the 'needs' of workers; in 1977 we spoke of proletarian 'desire'. Today, however, you propose neither need nor desire as the affective core of an ontology of being-in-common, but love. To what extent is this series of mutations, from need to desire to love, historically determined?

AN   What we have tried to do (in what is also a polemical gesture) is give the concept of love a strongly anti-religious, anti-idealist and anti-psychoanalytic tonality. We are therefore opposed to the isolation of love from the ontological totality. But we also try to conceive of it in Spinozian terms; that is, not only as the supreme accomplishment of knowledge but also as a force that traverses the terrain that moves from needs to desires. Love, for us, is attached to desire, in all its forms and with all its powers. This is why this new quality cannot be evaluated in terms of psychological drives or analytic libido but as a force of cohesion and construction of the common. Love is a fleeing from solitude, from individualism, not for religious, idealist or psychoanalytic reasons but through open and powerful dispositifs. From this point of view, having recourse to Deleuze and Guattari is fundamental. Here 'love' is… I would no longer call it love but collective and constitutive force: an attempt to bring the collective back to singularities and to grasp the way in which this ensemble of singularities becomes an institutional capacity, a capacity to be together, by way of love as a materialistic construction. With joy.

FDL/JES   This simultaneously political and ontological dimension of love is in tension with the tradition of political 'friendship' that begins with Aristotle and leads to Derrida. Love seems to be able to do without what is present in this other tradition, namely the concept of the enemy and enmity. Can love as an instrument of political struggle do without the figure of the enemy?

AN   No doubt. This is not really a Levinasian version of the recognition of the other. It is a material dimension of the common. Love and the common go together.

No, we have no need for an enemy, even if in our case love, being a force, can develop a destructive function – because, after all, the enemy exists.

FDL/JES   At the end of the chapter 'Beyond Capital?' you propose a series of 'reforms' to 'save capital' (p. 310), reforms that are 'necessary to biopolitical production' (p. 307), including education in the use of new technologies, opposition to the privatization of ideas, the proliferation of the instruments of participatory democracy and, above all, the introduction of a minimum guaranteed income.

The very idea that you would propose such reforms might seem regressive in the context of the more ample revolutionary strategy that your discourse as a whole implies. What is the rhetorical strategy behind these seemingly disconcerting proposals to 'save capital from itself'?

AN   You have to keep in mind that this book was written before Obama, during the Bush era. We could say that the *coup d'état* against empire failed, that from American unilateralism we would quickly pass on to more pluralistic forms of organization of globalization. After these things, written before the emergence of Obama on the political stage, comes the crisis. Now, these propositions might appear to be retrograde positions: we are however convinced that there are certain destructive limits that it is best capital not reach. There is, perhaps, in our discourse at this moment a syndicalist spirit, which is part of my old militant's bad taste. On the other hand, there is Michael's good sense, which is realist and sometimes attracted by my syndicalist overtures. The debate is always ample between us on these points, and these things do not get written easily. That said, if we stop with the jokes and return to our subject, I remain convinced that, in the rupture of the global capitalist process, in the rupture and bifurcation of systems of power and government, we must work on the inside. The problem is knowing how to manage the crisis, the rupture of capitalist development. All this leads us to seek out a path. It is less interesting to know if these paths are more or less feasible; what is important is to point out a route along which the revolution will not be an explosion somewhere down the road but can only be defined a posteriori. The revolution is not a boom but always a construction. It is in this sense that these propositions might seem – and in a certain sense are – retrograde. Not that much, though, if you take into account the moment in which this book was written. In fact, we see that Obama is not able to deliver what he promised, and it certainly wasn't the revolution. What is important is to repeat that the revolutionary process is always a construction, the product of a 'making the multitude'.

FDL/JES In recent years there has been an insistence on the dichotomy between the real economy and financial speculation. This seems to correspond to the two subjectivities you speak of: the multitude as productive force on the one side and a sterile and parasitic capital on the other. However, in your discussion of contemporary crises, you conclude with this question: 'Might the power of money (and the finance world in general) to represent the social field of production be, in the hands of the multitude, an instrument of freedom, with the capacity to overthrow misery and poverty?' (p. 295). In what sense is it possible to think money outside of its function as command and control of production and of the multitude as a productive force?

AN Before all of that, we should refer to the critical reflection on political economy carried out by researchers like Christian Marazzi, Carlo Vercellone and so on, and in general the entire 'regulation' school.[10] The first element to underline is that finance has become a central element of the production process. The traditional distinction between monetary policy on one side and the 'real' productive level on the other is an impossible distinction, politically and practically, from a point of view internal to economic processes. Today capitalism is ruled by rent. The large industrial firm, rather than reinvesting profit, banks on rent. The lifeblood of capital is today called rent, and this rent covers an essential function in the circulation of capital and maintenance of the capitalist system: maintenance of the social hierarchy and of the unity of the command of capital.

Money in this way becomes the sole measure of social production. In this way we have an ontological definition of money as form, blood, internal circulation, in which money as socially constructed value and as measure of the economic system is consolidated. Whence the total subordination of society to capital. Labour power, and thus the activity of society, is included in this money, which is at the same time measure, control and command. Politics dances on this rope.

If this is the situation, it is logical that the rupture – every rupture – take place in this frame. We should imagine – and I say this to provoke, but not only that – how it is possible today to form a soviet, that is, bring the struggle, force, the multitude, the common to bear in this new reality. The multitude is not simply exploited: it is exploited socially, just as the worker in the factory was. *Mutatis mutandis*, we can propose therefore the validity of the struggle over wages at the social level (of money). Capital is always a relation (between those who command and those who work), and it is in this relation that the subsumption of labour power into and under money is established. But this is also what determines the rupture.

The current crisis can be interpreted starting from these presuppositions. The crisis starts out from the necessity of maintaining order while multiplying money (the subprime loans and the entire mechanism these imply served to buy off the proletarians, to pay for social reproduction from the point of view of a capital and a banking system that dominate this world). It is therefore necessary to lay one's hands on this thing in order to destroy the capacities of capitalist direction. There can be no equivocation on this point. Many readings of this crisis have been proposed, but Marazzi's is the one to keep in mind, as we do ourselves in large part[11] – because here, unlike in all those formulations that locate the reasons for the crisis in the gap between finance and real production, there is an insistence on the fact that financialization is not simply an unproductive and parasitic deviation of surplus value and collective investment but the very form of accumulation of capital within new processes of social and cognitive production of value. The current financial crisis is therefore interpreted as a blockage of the accumulation of capital (on the proletarian side) and as the implosive result of a lack of capital accumulation.

How to get out of a crisis of this sort? Only by means of a social revolution. Today any new deal must consist in the construction of new rights of social ownership of common goods – a right that would be opposed to the right to private property. In other words, if up until now the access to a common good has taken the form of private debt, from now on it is legitimate to demand the same right in the form of social rent. Making these common rights recognized is the sole and correct way to get out of this crisis. Some (Rancière, Žižek and Badiou) will consider these reforms to be completely useless and costly for workers. Fine. Why don't we try them out? Why don't we propose them to Wall Street?

FDL/JES One of the classical critiques addressed to your previous books, *Empire* and *Multitude*, concerns the apparent tension between the hypothesis of the passage from a situation of formal to real subsumption, in which nothing can be produced outside capital because nothing is exterior to it, on the one hand, and the paradoxically 'external' (because sterile and parasitic) character of capital relative to biopolitical production.

In *Commonwealth* you speak of a more complex coexistence of mechanisms of subsumption, of a 'reciprocal movement also under way in the process of globalization, from the real subsumption to the formal, creating not new "outsides" to capital but severe divisions and hierarchies within the capitalist globe' (p. 230). There is no question of a return to the past but of the coexistence of diverse models in the 'striated geography' of contemporary capitalism, more in relation, for example, to the Marx of the sixth, unpublished chapter of Book 1 of *Capital*. Is this 'striated geography' a new phenomenon or a rereading of the hypotheses guiding your earlier works? In what manner do borders, for example, as well as migrations, territorializations, the flexibility and mobility of work – especially in the case of immigrants – play an increasingly important role in your analysis?

AN   We speak of a formal subsumption that is reappearing today, but in reality it is not reappearing. There has always been this ambiguity of diverse levels. The world itself is diverse and differentiated – the Chinese situation or the Bolivian situation... there is no doubt that these striations of the world exist!

As for the extreme deployment of the discourse on formal and real subsumption, as well as its immediate transference into the concept of biopower, this occurred in the 1990s, and even prior to this in my case. It was, in reality, a hypothesis guiding research, a way of undoing a set of ideas that had been consolidated and seemed fallacious to me. In the current context, in return, the attenuation of this extreme articulation allows for a deepening of the analysis, above all, obviously, when the problem becomes one of organization, and therefore of the capacity to adapt the analysis to diverse terrains in order to be able to stay close to these diverse realities. I have always been a little scared of these things, because I know that opportunism is always lying in wait whenever we speak of adapting thoughts to diversity. There are those who say that you should be attentive to the zones of formal subsumption and then, on the basis of these lovely preoccupations, change the script. Just look, for example, at the re-emergence today of the strong Eurocentrism when it comes to debates about ecology, where we often encounter Eurocentric attitudes.

We must, then, always be attentive to discourses on these subjects, for we too easily pass from one terrain to another. On the terrain of political economy and modes of government, the discourse on formal and real subsumption continues to function as the key to understanding them. It will no doubt have to be rearticulated from the perspective of a strategy for constructing political objectives, as well as from the perspective of tactics and practice, for it is clear that formal and real subsumption will have very different effects on the dynamics of governance.

As for migrations and immigrant labour, these themes are becoming increasingly central. Immigration represents a tendency, and when we speak of cognitive and mobile labour we realize that the figure of the immigrant is closely related to the new form of work. It is not simply a residue, a background noise. It is the true nature of work. In this modification we encounter lots of problems but, just as much, we find the possibility for another happiness.

FDL/JES On the basis of this novel aspect, *Commonwealth* would seem to introduce a nuance into another critique aimed at your earlier works, namely a supposed underestimation, both quantitative and qualitative, of the role played by forms of material labour in relation to a new cognitive labour. In *Commonwealth*, however, you seem at times to maintain this prevalence of immaterial labour over more traditional forms of work (and the corresponding forms of exploitation). In what sense is the affirmation of biopolitical production a synonym, for you, of the priority – tendential, say – of immaterial and cognitive labour over other forms of production?

AN I don't know if we managed to explain it, but there is no doubt that when we speak today of cognitive work we speak of it in the terms that I used at the beginning of the interview; that is, not only as the central hegemonic element in the production of value but also as the consolidation of all the vices of material labour and all the difficulties endured in the past (alienation, fragmentation, fatigue, etc.) that are found in the cognitive worker as well. The cognitive worker is not a privileged worker. He or she is in certain ways, because he or she does not have dirty hands or a dirty shirt, but this hardly means the exploitation has diminished. He or she is still concretely rooted in *bios*, and the body suffers physically. This means that we should have a realistic and complex image of work, and therefore that liberation concerns not only fatigue but all those aspects that hurt not only the body but the mind or spirit as well: physical, mental and, above all, social aspects. Let's take up the theme of debt, for example, the fact that you should live on the basis of debt, on this damned credit card. Already in the 1980s, when I began to investigate precarious labour, I began to see the same type of problem. It was the first encounter with cognitive work I had. All the conditions of the precarity of work and of forms of life were already there.

When we spoke of cognitive labour, then, we never spoke of a labour in which there is no suffering. The criticisms directed at us have been unjust. But the problem is not there. They attack us because a lot of our comrades, nostalgic for the old images of worker power, do not acknowledge immaterial–cognitive labour's capacity for resistance and rebellion. The privilege of cognitive labour consists in the fact that the means of work, intelligence, is not consumed in the work process and is immediately common. Will we succeed in transforming this community into a common revolutionary weapon?

To conclude, allow me to insist on two other themes that, in my opinion, are central in Commonwealth, themes we have not yet addressed.

The first is the polemic against every sort of identity politics and – even before all politics – against every metaphysics or ideology of identity, described as an organic or natural presupposition. For us, all drives to identity are the plague of thought and of political practices: from nationalism to patriotism and to racism, from fundamentalism to ecological localism, from possessive individualism to syndicalist corporatism, and let's not forget sexism or the religion of the family: yes, precisely this institution of the family that liberalism, the state and Hegel consider the basis of civil society. It seems to us that, after the withering of civil society, on which we insisted in *Empire* and *Multitude*, we should follow with the extinction of the family as the basis of naturalist sexism and of every other juridical institution based on the private. The cooperative intersection that we recognize in cognitive labour power and its mobility is opposed to any identity that would want to represent itself as a subject. We have spent a lot of time recognizing that the multitude is an ensemble of singularities. But every singularity is equally a multitude.

The second theme is poverty. If the necessity of bifurcation imposes itself on capital, as well as that of recognizing the rupturing of the dialectical process that constitutes it, then constant capital and capitalist management find themselves on one side, labour power and variable capital on the other. Whence the first consequence of bifurcation: an unlimited augmentation of poverty. Like suffering, poverty is now part of the coerciveness of work. It's an ineluctable passage, a terrible one, for whoever analyses the current conditions of the proletariat, but also for those who militate for the communist cause. Militating with and among the poor has become, today, fundamental. Proletarians, workers, the precarious, they are all poor. But, included as the poor of biopower, the poor are not simply excluded: poverty – in the global world, in the world of social production – is always inclusion, an inherence in a relation to capital that invests society and puts it to work. In the biopolitical relation, the existence of the poor must be considered in its entirety. We think that in these conditions the revolts of the poor, real jacqueries, are today events that occur and present themselves as inevitable comings; they are due in order to construct a constitutive terrain, a political opening for the forces struggling against capitalist domination, that is, for the construction of a free commonwealth.

11

On the Institutions of the Common

Prolegomena for a Constituent Inquiry*

With Judith Revel

TONI Opening the discussion on the institutions of the common, I would like to retrace an experience that was fundamental for me: that of the Comitato Operaio di Porto Marghera [Porto Marghera Workers' Committee]. Porto Marghera was an industrial centre that grew alongside Venice between the two wars. It contained primary processing, engineering and chemical factories. The beginning of the 1960s saw the opening of the Petrolchimico plant, which initiated a technologically renewal throughout a kombinat. Soon Petrolchimico had 15,000 direct workers and almost as many in its associated industries. The Porto Marghera district, which comprised the original Zone One and Zone Two, established around the Petrolchimico plant, soon reached 60,000 workers. The intervention of the comrades from Potere Operaio [PO; Workers' Power], the political group of which I was a member, was already operational at the end of the 1950s, and it was about to become decisive in the class struggle events of the 1960s through the construction of the Workers' Committee. What was the Workers' Committee? It was an *institution of the common*.

The qualitative leap came when we began to organize at the Petrolchimico plant, at Sice, and at Chatillon, a large factory subsidiary to Petrolchimico. We did this after the first mass strike at Petrolchimico in 1963, which was a struggle against the reduction of holiday entitlements. That morning, it was reported,

---

* Originally published under the title 'Sulle istituzioni del comune: prolegomeni per un' inchiesta costituente: conversazione fra Toni Negri e Judith Revel', *Uninomade*/Esc, Rome, 15 February 2008.

the workers stayed outside the plant 'spontaneously': there were 5,000 of them on the *campaccio*.* When production stopped, the accumulated gases coming out of the chimneys flared up at dawn with a flame that illuminated Marghera and the whole of the Venetian lagoon in a way never seen since. *That moment was the beginning of workers' autonomy.* The workers, together with the militants of PO, embarked on an active working-class research investigation [*inchiesta*], that is, a detailed analysis of the cycle of production in the factories concerned. At the same time the Marghera Workers' Committee was established. This brought together representatives from the Petrochimico plant and the adjacent factories. Many of them were members of various trade union bodies; some were also members of political parties (both the Socialist Party and the Communist Party). The Committee met at least once a week in open assembly, but comrades from the factories and students who were coming from Padua or Venice could be found in its office almost every day. Note that this was the period from 1962 to 1967, during which working-class autonomy organized its own political line: a discourse that was systematically verified in discussions on the shop floor, in confrontation with the trade unions at plant level and, when possible, also in confrontation with various levels in the provincial organization of the Communist Party and the Socialist Party. It goes without saying that, especially in the first years of activity of the Workers' Committee, the clash with the trade unions and political organizations in the older Zone One was very strong. In Zone Two it was less problematic, but still solid. Occasionally this clash would end up in scuffles at the factory gates; unfortunately developing an open and productive discussion was possible much less often. Very early on, the trade union and political hierarchies declared a ban on the forces of autonomy. The language was Stalinist: we were described as 'provocateurs and fascists'! It was only when the Committee began to manage the struggle directly – and thus to exclude from it the trade union and party leadership – that the latter sought contact and discussion. But by then we were on the verge of 1968.

Gradually, however, the differences between the lines of organization and struggle proposed by the Committee and the lines of action proposed by the union started to be apparent and became

---

* A rough patch of land.

more sharply antagonistic. But this was not just a matter of tactical alternatives. In the Committee we asked ourselves more and more frequently what it meant to exercise counterpower in the factory and whether the workers' idea of power could be homologated to that of the boss – which was basically what was preached by the 'productivist' union and party officials. Workers began to question the organization of the working day: was it right to have to go to work every day for a living? And then there was the denunciation of the 'death regime' – the insane health hazards that loomed everywhere in the chemical factories. Every so often someone would bring to the Committee office a cage containing a mouse or a canary that had died because of gas leaks in the factory. The cages were kept at the workers' feet because, when there was a leak, the gas accumulated at ground level. The mouse dies, but the worker can escape. As a result, the alternatives to the union strategy – a strategy that aimed simply to bring about further development – were getting stronger and stronger and the discourse regarding the refusal of work began to circulate as an effective organizing tool. It was clear that here the Committee was bringing into the struggle a behaviour-related option that went far beyond the trade unionist and socialist conception of development in the exercise of command; in particular, it went against the idea that Italian Communist Party hierarchies and trade union bureaucracies might simply replace the bosses. It was this 'real socialism' – not only in the Soviet version but in the Togliattian version, in fact especially there – that was called into question. The consequences of this choice would become fully apparent after 1968, during the course of the 1970s.

The Workers' Committee in the 1960s embodied a paradox. On the one hand, it was building, or in any case facilitating, general conditions of rooting, development, extension and trade unionism – especially in a region such as the Veneto, where the labour movement was very underdeveloped; on the other hand, it was building the conditions for a political break with the official labour movement – and this was to become decisive for the movement's own destiny in the years that followed. The break took place especially on the terrain of the organization of the struggle. We wanted incisive struggles, of the kind that hurt the bosses; and we also wanted to have direct effects on the corporate and national economy. An initial platform of struggle objectives was established. The issue was not only quantitative: apart from wage rises, there were also increasing trends towards egalitarianism (e.g. the famous

5,000 lire, equal for all workers, from the first to the last; and we should recall that in 1969 this demand was transmitted from Porto Marghera to the Workers' Committees of the Fiat factories in Turin). Other demands aimed at reducing the number of working hours (e.g. new structures were designed for a 36-hour working week) and at recomposing all the sectors and strata of the class (e.g. the struggle to take on the books workers from the subsidiary companies and also precarious workers). The other essential issue, always present among workers' demands, was, as I mentioned, health and safety at work. After the condemnation that even the Court of the Italian Republic has been obliged to express over the shameful delay related to the countless murders committed by Petrolchimico in the past thirty years, perhaps today it can be publicly stated that the union's monetization of health hazards was a criminal policy. The Committee had understood this right from the start, and the cross with a mannequin on it that wears a gas mask – that crucifix that was raised in front of the main gates of the Petrolchimico plant – remains as a shocking reminder. It also symbolizes a consciousness of struggle the likes of which we have not seen since.

The Workers' Committee was a real *institution of the common*. Its history can be read as the story of the genesis of a new power. So here I would like to open reflection on the definition of the autonomous workers' institution (AWI) – a definition that will have to be discussed when we begin to write the history of the Workers' Committees of Porto Marghera as an institution, as well as the history of its actions between the 1960s and 1970s.

What I mean in this context by an 'autonomous institution of workers' is an organization characterized by

(a) the workers' *independent* ability to propose themes of struggle and a consequent and coordinated indication of instrumental actions, and thus AWI's own *normative* capacity;

(b) an autonomous capacity to *organize* and manage wage and political struggles in a significant industrial and social sector, and thus an autonomous capacity to *exercise force* in support of organized action;

(c) the success of the *struggle for recognition* from other institutions (trade union and political, of the labour movement and of the employers) within the same industrial and social sector, and therefore a certain *social legitimation of AWI's normative capacity and use of force*.

If we want to deepen this characterization, we would have to show how the normative capacity of the AWI is formed through self-learning processes *from the bottom up*, by moving from the political and technological experience of the workers towards an alternative conceptualization and projectuality and from linguistic production to the construction of one (or several) matching forms of praxis. When I speak of the organizational capacity of the AWI I mean *collective intelligence* already implicit in the processes of self-formation, which considers the *workers' inquiry* [inchiesta operaia] or, better still, co-research as a basis for the construction of common concepts that can be transformed into dispositifs of action.

As for political legitimacy, on the one hand the AWI recognizes itself as an *instituent* capacity, in other words as being reflexive and tendentially normative, and on the other hand, from a political point of view, it affirms itself as a *constituent* power [*potenza*] and can develop into a political subject. For more than a century now, both law and the political sociology of labour – from Sinzheimer to Eugen Ehrlich, without leaving out the theory of soviets, especially in its Luxemburg formulation – have indicated the productivity of these definitions.

But all this took place in the Fordist era, when the factory was the privileged location of the revolutionary experience. What does the AWI become, in the transition from Fordism to post-Fordism and to a new mode of production? It has to become an institution that is even more open to the common than it was in the former, Fordist mode of production, since the mode of production is now more common. We therefore hypothesize a new institution: an autonomous common institution (ACI) or autonomous multitudinous organization (AMO).

This new institution is located on the relational horizon (communicational, informational, etc.), which is characteristic of the new mode of production. This horizontal dimension is further characterized by its being networked. The network comes to be the basis of the new common institution. At this point, however, it will not be easy to recognize, within this transition and within this new formation, characteristics of *autonomy* in the sense indicated above. The ACI can indeed be defined as an *expansive* and *networked* institution, but another side of it will reveal itself to be a dissipative force. When the outer perimeter of the factory gives way, when the given spaces of exploitation of labour power are exceeded, when the whole of civil society is put to work, every common institution risks seeing its own (exodic) expansive form destroyed and dissolved in the mass. As a result, that first element of institutionality (networked, exodic) risks lacking any specifically *normative* characteristic: this means that no element is present that might enable us to focus, alongside the recognition of the horizontal dimension, on a *vertical* passage, established on the basis of an autonomous organizational capacity and effective recognition by other institutions – hence by a self-legitimating power.

I offer a philosophical hypothesis. Any kind of institution and government, from the most concentrated to the most diffuse, is always based on a relationship between forces that develop genealogically, along a horizontal dimension, and then find themselves in a vertical relationship. I could add that any definition of 'public institution' is given as a balance point on a right-angled plot that places networked consensus [*consenso reticolare*] and adhesion to the structure on the x axis (i.e. the horizontal line) and networked consensus and the exercise of command on the y axis (i.e. the vertical line). The definition of 'public institution' as fixing a point on this plot chart is obviously exposed to a series of quantitative and qualitative *differentials*, both on the y axis of cohesion and on the x axis of command. In the schema that I have described, the public appears as a moment of equilibrium between the networked set of singularities reduced to epistemic unity on the ordinate axis and the concentration of force established on the vertical axis.

Now, this definition of 'public institution' is unsatisfactory from the point of view of the ACI because it fails to represent the expansive moment of the network – *that which is proper to living labour*. It captures the exodus, so to speak, only in its *intensive* dimension. To put it better, this definition fails to transfer the *expansive* power of the singularities from the forms of resistance to the modes of decision, or rather from episteme to ontology; in short, it fails to *form force*.

JUDITH To find a solution to this problem, let us start from the established fact that a transformation of the mode of production is a given. If one looks at this transformation from the point of view of what is usually called the 'technical composition' of labour, *production has become a common* – and, tendentially, a highly cooperative one. From the point of view of the political composition of labour, it would then be necessary for this common composition to be matched by new political and juridical categories, capable of organizing the common, of stating its centrality, of describing its new figures and its internal functioning. Now, these new categories do not exist – *and we miss them*. The fact that it is possible to mask the new insurgencies of the common and that we continue to think in obsolete terms, as if the place of overall production were still only the factory, or as if the network were nothing more than a flat figure of communication… in sum, the fact that we continue to act as if nothing had changed about the technical composition of labour power – this is the most perverse of all the mystifications of power.

This mystification rests especially on the ideological reproposal of two terms that function as lures and cages, as fictions and illusions, but that at the same time correspond to two ways of appropriating the common of humans. The first of these terms resorts to the category of 'private'; the second resorts to the category of 'public'. In the first case, property – as defined by Rousseau: and the first man who said 'this is mine…' – is an appropriation of the common by one only; it is an expropriation of all the others. Today *private property* consists precisely in denying people *their common right* over what only their cooperation is capable of producing.

The second category that concerns me here is that of the 'public'. The reasoning of good old Rousseau, who was so hard on private property, rightly making it the source of all corruption and human suffering, breaks down at this point. Problem of the social contract, problem of modern democracy: since private property generates inequality, how can we invent a political system where everything, while belonging to everyone, nevertheless belongs to no one? *N'appartienne pourtant à personne…* The trap closes on Jean-Jacques, but it also closes on us. In fact this is what 'the public' is: what belongs to everyone but belongs to nobody, in other words what belongs to the state. And, since we should be the state (which obviously we are not – especially when we can't get to the end of the month…), they have to invent something to sweeten the pill of its having laid hands upon the common. In other words, we have to be made to believe that the state represents us and that, if it arrogates to itself rights over what we produce, it does so because that 'we' (which we actually are) is not what we produce *in common* and what we invent and organize *as a common*, but is what allows us to exist. The common, the state tells us, does not belong to us, since we do not really create it: the common is our soil, our foundation, what we have under our feet: our *nature*, our *identity*. And if that common does not really belong to us – because *to be* is not *to have* – the state's laying hands on the common will not be called appropriation or exploitation, but (economic) management and political and delegation representation. QED: the implacable beauty of political pragmatism, the transformation of what we are, that is, common, into nature and into identity.

At this point we can readdress the *formal presentation of the Cartesian coordinates* on which we reopened the discussion: that formal presentation needs to be open to examination.

(a) First of all, that form is, as we have seen, very real. That point of balance is a utopia of power, an attempt to castrate the *common* in order to reduce it to a *set of privations*, to a *model of the private that is called 'public'*. Here we find the reactionary tendencies that are nested in democracy – continuity of property and the rhetorical tradition of individualism; habitus (*à la* Bourdieu) in the ruling classes and the habit of banal life; exception, not as the mythology of an extreme and exasperated power but as the expression of a full power, nourished by all pre-existing law and customs: extremism of the centre (Göring's beautiful industrial and military dispositifs rather than the madness of Hitler). That balance is therefore very real and is immediately our enemy, just as all the (more or less) transcendental or religious coordinates are our enemies, from ecclesiastical natural law to the blabberings of the *kathēkon*.

(b) Secondly, that *form* is contradictory in itself, because, in order to prevent the network of relations from shifting its expressive and cooperative potential from the horizontal level to the vertical level of power, it is forced to negate any possibility of translation, and therefore any power of singularity. In other words, it is forced to deny not only the relational, cooperative element but also the innovative one, which resides in the *biopolitical* determination of the network. The naturalist and identitarian hypostases find here the most suitable place for them to become fixed.

(c) For us, then, *nature* and *identity* are mystifications of the modern paradigm of power. *To regain possession of our common*, we first have to produce a drastic critique of these mystifications. *We are in no sense participants in them; and we do not want to be part of them.* 'We': that is not an essence, a 'thing' of which it is necessary to proclaim that it is 'public'. Our common, on the contrary, is not our foundation; rather it is production, an invention that is always restarted. 'We' is the name of a horizon, the name of a becoming. The common is always before us; it is a process. *We are this common*: doing, producing, participating, moving, sharing, circulating, enriching, inventing, relaunching and so on.

For nearly three centuries, we have thought of democracy as the administration of public affairs – that is, as the institutionalization of the state's appropriation of the common. Today democracy can be thought of only in radically different terms: as the common management of the common. This management implies a redefinition of space as *networked* (without limits; but this does not mean without hierarchies and internal borders, to the point of cosmopolitanism) and a redefinition of temporality as *constituent*. There is no question now of defining a sort of contract that ensures that *everything, belonging to everyone, nevertheless belongs to no one.* No: *everything, being produced by everyone, belongs to everyone.*

TONI It is quite evident from the foregoing that this 'belonging to all' is a becoming. It is the very process of constitution of the institutions of the multitude, in their dynamic, which is non-teleological – a finality constructed through dispositifs that are productive within a chaotic whole cannot be defined as teleological – but rather 'dys-utopic'.

In fact there is no possible prefiguration of the institutions of the common if we do not recognize that a constituent power is in action. This opens up some other problems that cannot be underestimated, given the temporal and ontological pre-eminence that we have attributed to constituent power since we saw it in action in the AWI.

On the other hand, in the mainstream* literature, constituent power is primarily considered to be a juridical category. This *potenza* is trapped (and in fact definitively castrated) by public law. How can one retrieve it? Of course, historical analysis remains fundamental and shows us how constituent power, whenever it has exploded, has had ontological effects – creative and libertarian. But I am not interested here in a critical history of law; I am concerned to identify the political dispositif, the latent and expressive intentionality of constituent power [*potere*] as a machine that produces institution in the current conjuncture – in other words as a machine to be used for the construction of a common law [*diritto comune*] against public law [*diritto pubblico*]. Raising the matter of institutions of the common in these terms becomes a question of

---

* 'mainstream' in English in the original.

affirming constituent power as a permanent, internal source of the process of political–juridical constitution of society.

(a) In this research, the relationships that social movements impose on governments and the material determinations that movements express in constitutional arrangements have to be evaluated. Constituent power as an *internal source* of public and constitutional law was especially evident in the new constitutions of Latin America in the twenty years after the 1990s: it determines entirely novel relationships and new constitutional dynamics in terms of both government and governance, thus reactivating the *common law of the multitudes* that has hitherto been excluded from power and transforming the entire ideal-type fabric of the democratic constitution.

(b) In this research, the temporalities that implicitly or explicitly link the action of movements to constitutional determinations must also be analysed afresh. When we look at the new dynamics that have linked multitudinous forms and institutional arrangements in the transition processes that take place in new economic areas (China, India, Brazil, etc.), we have to recognize that new institutional figures are being born in the experiences of postcoloniality, and these figures cannot be brought back to the models of European modernity.

But note that these research indications arise also from the objective analysis of the chaotic situation in which public institutions find themselves today, both in Europe and in the United States, which means in the states of capitalist modernity. Advance signals and traces of constituent *potenza* are to be found in the crisis into which the public institutions have been plunged. In this regard, case studies could be constructed that concentrate on the highest peaks of critical and self-critical analysis in the legal sciences (Teubner and the new course of legal institutionalism) and in the social sciences (Boltanski and the new course of sociological institutionalism). I believe that, in order to remodel the issue and redefine a possible ideal type of institutions of the common, we have to reopen and reinvent the inquiry [*inchiesta*] and make it address various aspects of the new capitalist constitution of the social.

Here is, then, what we have to assume in this phase of inquiry:

(1) *cognitive capital* as a characteristic of the valorization process;
(2) *the metropolis* as a new focal point of exploitation;

(3) *finance capital* as a new figure of overall capital, or rather of the command form: Christus–fiscus, this really was a terrain of antagonistic investigation (Christus–subprimes, etc.);*
(4) boundaries, hierarchies and fragmentations as an *analytics of the multitude* (and possibly of war);
(5) *the understanding* of struggles and institutions as a terrain of possible political 'dys-utopia'.

The *constituent inquiry* has the capacity to define the political method of critical analysis and militant insubordination at this stage. So here we have a new algebraic table (considering that everything happens in the network) that will perhaps allow us to grasp the element of innovation between the humps and the differences that the network itself proposes. But if the geometry of the multitude cannot be flattened on that of the network, the geometry of the revolution will probably correspond to the geometry of the institutions of the common. In any event, this is the hypothesis that the constituent inquiry will have to assume as it proceeds on its course.

---

* This is a reference to the Latin tag *Quod non capit Christus, rapit fiscus*: 'What Christ does not receive, the exchequer seizes'.

Part IV

In Conclusion

Part IV

Conclusion

12
From the Commune to the Common*

The Commune as a historical event

Let us begin with the Paris Commune as a historical event. What is your thinking as to what the Commune meant in that historical moment, as an event of its time? How did Marx read the Commune? And what kind of transformations did it produce in political thought, and also in the workers' movement?

It is such a formidable event, but at the same time so complex, that it is always difficult to define it. There are two books, one old and one new, that offer a starting point: at one end, *Histoire de la Commune de 1871*, Prosper-Olivier Lissagaray's old book, the most important and most objective thing ever written about the Commune, written with the freshness of a fighter and the truth of a refugee from the Commune itself; at the other end, *Common Luxury*, Kristin Ross's new book, which is the most recent offering on the subject. Ross's book arose from an academic thesis on the poet Arthur Rimbaud that starts from that impressive poem, 'L'orgie parisienne ou Paris se repeuple' ('The Parisian orgy, or Paris is re-peopled'), written during the bloody week [*la semaine sanglante*] – the week in which the Commune was massacred by the victors of Versailles.

There is a particularly beautiful verse that I recall:

Quand tes pieds ont dansé si fort dans les colères
Paris! Quand tu reçus tant de coups de couteau,

---

* First published as 'Dalla comune al comune', interview with Niccolò Cuppini, *Euronomade* 2.0, 16 March 2021.

Quand tu gis, retenant dans tes prunelles claires
Un peu de la bonté du fauve renouveau
[When your feet danced so vigorously in anger,
Paris! When you received so many knife cuts,
when you lay, keeping in your clear pupils
a little of the goodness of the fawn renewed]

What a powerful recollection of that communist uprising! These are lines to which I am really attached. I used them in an interview, 'Dominio e sabotaggio' ('Domination and Sabotage'). In that poem Paris is revolutionary madness. Paris the madwoman. Paris is the martyr, under the knives of Versailles, of a mad and wild renewal. *Fauve* – 'wild' – sums it all up.

The Commune is the event par excellence, in every sense. On the one hand, because around the insurrection there was an accumulation of most of the forces that had organized themselves in the preceding fifty years – starting from the 1830s, the years described in Victor Hugo's *Les Misérables*, and thus from the rise of 'subversive liberalism' against the Restoration. On the other hand, the Commune was the product of the affirmation and consolidation of corporations of workers in struggle – the same corporations that had made a first organized appearance in the revolutionary and armed struggles of June 1848. For instance, the building of barricades was a new experiment in citizen architecture – and is recounted in *Les Misérables*, by the way (a book that I recently reread, I don't even know why; I was done studying, so I plunged into these thousands of pages and read them all, even the really boring bits, for instance those pages on the techniques of building barricades, which is not the easiest thing to do). So the Parisian proletariat was behind barricades, and this terrified the bosses.

There, in the Commune, there was a democratic–radical expansion of the socialism of the workers' movement. And alongside this process ran another line, namely the consolidation of intellectual and proletarian energies in struggle – a foundation of communism for the centuries to come. We know its consequences on establishing the importance of this experience in its most revolutionary form, when it was to be rescued through the reflection of Marx and others.

This experience was organized around the two elements that are still present and by now classic in the action of communists: on the one hand, the quest for a progressive democracy that goes beyond representation and defines itself as council-based democracy, direct democracy, immediately participative democracy. This is the first element; and, as a consequence of this radicality, the revocability of mandates, the payment of wages for the roles undertaken – just a median wage, one would say the wage for necessary social labour; and by this token the representatives become simple mandataries, controlled for the duration of their function and on an equal footing with those whom they represent: this is direct democracy. On the other hand there is the issue of wages in production and reproduction, where political participation must reveal its abstract presupposition – namely the fact of productive cooperation – and repay it concretely, through a redistribution of profit, even if in the legislative dynamics of the Commune this is put in a very narrow perspective. This is because in reality there was just a reduction in the working hours of bakers: previously they worked all night, whereas now a reduced working time is applied; this reform signals the attention that was paid to conditions of work and to wages and income during the Commune, short-lived as it was.

In the history of the Commune, these two elements – direct democracy and income for all – will combine in singular forms, as especially Kristin Ross has highlighted. This does not arise simply from the involvement of a democratic intellectual class in the proletarian Commune and its management, but from the investment that the Commune extends over daily life: today we identify here its *biopolitical* character. This seems fundamental to me. A question from the working citizens arises here, and is put in very progressive terms: how can people manage to live together? How can people live together as if they were partying? Being together means having the possibility to be so, freely and equally, and also in exuberant form, with equally shared possibilities, and thus having the possibility to form our common passions under the sign of happiness. Here you are: this seems to me to be the historically exceptional and unique form of the Commune.

So let's go back to what the Commune actually represented in its own time. In Paris, 1871 was also a year of resistance. We should not forget that the Prussian army was still surrounding the city and that the Prussians had made peace with the versaillais* who were under the walls... but the Prussian army was still behind, by the side [*à côté*]. So, for the Commune, it was not just a matter of fighting but also of fighting against the Prussians. It was no coincidence that in 1871

---

* The *versaillais* (lit. 'residents of Versailles') were members of the political coalition that suppressed the Commune in 1871.

the Garibaldians, too, joined the fight against the Prussians. Around Belfort, in the borderlands between Switzerland and France, in the lower Rhineland, the bands of Garibaldians were the only ones that kept the Germans in check, bringing the voice of the Commune there too. Almost everyone, from Garibaldians to anarchists, was fighting for the Commune and against the Prussians and the *versaillais*; and then the anarchists easily adopted the model of the Commune, carrying it all the way through to the Marxists. But I think that, for the Commune to stand out with the brilliance it acquired, it took the workers' movement, as it came into being through the theoretical action of Marx. Yet the Marxists actually took this event in a completely different direction from the anarchists; or maybe not? Maybe the Commune functions as a matrix of all lineages, of all races, of all genders? The Commune, to put it in the language of Spinoza, is like the substance from which all the ways of being communist emerge. For me, this is what it represents.

The Commune over time

Let us move on in history. How did the Commune event reverberate in the workers' movement and in the other workers' movements? There is a story of Lenin dancing in the snow-covered square when the Russian Revolution had outlasted the Commune in number of days. But we should also think of the political imaginary in France in 1968 and of the writings of Lefebvre. Or perhaps I could ask whether, in your own experience of the Italian movement of 1977, there were references, anchorings to the Commune and, more generally, how the Commune has worked as a political theory and as an imaginary that it has itself sedimented.

When Lenin celebrated having surpassed the days of the Commune he was still in Petrograd. He still had to conquer the whole of Russia. And this was undoubtedly a revival, engineered by Lenìn (I still say Lenìn, with the Emilian pronunciation, as the older members of my family used to say it), of what Marx had built: *the Commune as an example of the extinction of the state.* This is where the universality of that slogan was established. By establishing a continuity with anarchism, Lenìn – but perhaps already Marx – posits 'taking the state' as a *tactical* moment vis-à-vis the communists' *strategy*, which is still that of the abolition of the state. For anarchists, the tactical moment is a transition of little account: taking the state is not followed by a period of transition – the state is destroyed and that's it. For Lenìn (and also for

Marx), on the other hand, there is instead a period of transition, when obviously enormous problems arise; this is all the more visible today after what happened in the Soviet Union, when the so-called period of extinction of the state became a terrible Stalinist mechanism of centralization of the state itself. What happened there has obviously created some problems for the Marxian theory of the state, precisely as regards its extinction! However, I am interested in the communard theme of the extinction of the state – and I say this in a radical way. I don't think it possible to call oneself a communist if one gives up on this concept. Of course, the extinction proposal has to be taken as a theoretical and practical task, and thus – to cast it in Weber's language – without any devaluation of the institutional realities and centralization functions typical of the complexity of the intertwinings between state and capitalism and of the processes of equalization that occur in the great transformations of social, economic and civil life, where cooperation has become both more widespread and more intensive. Just as happens today.

But at the very moment when these needs and urgencies are taken into account, there is also – as a duty in a radical ethics – the commitment to destroy any idea that the state has a monopoly on legitimate violence. Let us say it clearly: to destroy the very concept of legitimacy of power and to introduce the idea of the possibility of a plural dispositif of powers, of councils, of articulations that implement the dissolution of capitalist complexity and maintain command over this dissolution – these are the stakes to which all communist issues must yield and with which they have to play. This is true all the more today, when the discourse on class struggle and the state focuses with increasing resolution on a hypothesis and a theory of counterpower in action, a counterpower capable of producing the extinction of the central moment of power – the one clustered in the state.

There remains the problem of what a transition should be: from A to... what? Probably the very formula of the transition will constitute the social form of communist organization, and hence the form of that activity of constructing an interlacement of powers with which and through which it will be possible to affirm the maximum of freedom and the maximum of equality – and, of course, the maximum of productivity in its adaptation to the general conditions (physical and ecological) of survival of the human community.

Having said this, when we return to the Commune and to the two dynamics I mentioned earlier, the theme of the councils and the theme of equal wages are fully present throughout the communist experience. They live first of all in Lenin. I like to dig into what Lenin says – and it seems clear to me that, when he says 'soviets + electricity', he is saying exactly this: soviets as destruction of the state; and replacement of the state's functions by a regime of councils. On the other hand, he is saying electricity, which in that phase is the way to produce conditions for wage earners, the way to produce wealth, the way to give life to those who are to participate in power and in the survival of all. In communal life, life always precedes power – always, every single time. The Commune is central on account of this indication alone.

As regards Lefebvre... He is very important as a writer, even if, in my view, in order to judge him we need to dig a little deeper into the great polemics of the post-war period – those on Marxian humanism in particular – in which he fell foul of the French Communist Party and was thrown out by Althusser. We need to dig a little because recovering a certain version of communist humanism, probably with Lefebvre's help, remains a central task for me. Kristin Ross's book, behind all its postmodern elegances, actually extricates this Lefebvrian element – the humanism of the Commune as well as the humanism of the early Marx – from obtuse and ancient polemic. We should be careful here, because – it has to be admitted! – when Lefebvre dealt with the early Marx, he did it too much with the connivance of what had been a reactionary fashion at the beginning of the post-war period. In this framework, the humanism of Marx's writings of 1844 was invoked polemically against Marx's stance in *Capital*. In Italy it was Norberto Bobbio who became the hero of the 1844 Marx, naturally flirting with Roderigo di Castiglia (Togliatti's pseudonym in the magazine *Rinascita*). In Germany there was Iring Feschter, a colossal revisionist, well supported by the reactionary soul of the entire Frankfurt School. Lefebvre got caught up in this game and, since the French Communist Party was not as nice as the Italian Communist Party, he was not treated with kid gloves, like Bobbio, but was isolated and shamefully expelled from the party. Much to the contrary, Althusser interprets the 'pure Marx' against the youthful Marx, the logician against the humanist, and makes room for a caesura by virtue of which Marx became a materialist Marxist only after 1848. Neither interpretation is correct, as we know. But politics is above the truth! Lefebvre was half right, but got caught up in a bigger game and paid the price, because despite being undoubtedly the most intelligent person in the French Communist Party, despite being open to biopolitical humanism, to the analysis of ways of life and to the invention of a new materialist phenomenology of living in common, and despite making one of the most important contributions to our whole experience and analytical skills as communists – despite all this, he was cut off from the very entourage that interested him most.

And what is there to say about the Commune and the Italian movement of 1977? That movement could be seen as part of the tradition of the Commune. But 1977 was very ignorant. It was really dumb; its sources were comics. However, it is beyond doubt that 1977, in its ludic and political expressions and in the organization of its spaces – another very recent theme, the spatiality of movements – was part of this tradition. The space of the Commune, too, was in some ways the space of the streets and of the barricades, the space to which Haussmann would respond with his urban reform... which was designed to carve out this space and make it horizontal, like the firing of machine guns, and by so doing to make it less viable for the proletariat. And yet the space of the Commune was, and still is, the space of workers' organizations [*corporazioni*] and of shopkeepers, a pre-established space. Since it seems to me that research and polemics among urban thinkers have recently concentrated around the preconstituted space or the newly constituted, neo-constituted space, I completely agree that the theme of the neo-constituted space is fundamental to thinking about struggles and movements; but I have a hard time finding it in the historical past – probably down to 1977. In my own experience, among the communard spaces in Milan, only the Ticinese neighbourhood could have been described like that to some extent; or probably, on occasion, Quarto Oggiaro or Giambellino. And in Rome this level was reached only rarely (I am thinking of Trastevere, of the attacks on the Nixon cavalcade, for example). But it didn't go beyond that, whereas later on things changed: one begins to think of such spaces in Seattle in 1999, and they appear in full light in the great struggles of the 2011 cycle, in the Arab revolts and in Spain's Puerta del Sol uprising. This idea of the spatiality of movements obviously creates important organizational problems. I tried to study them with Michael Hardt in *Assembly*, but I don't think we were able to give a sense of what it means deep down. We took on this leitmotif, this refrain of 'Go...', of 'Call and respond'* – a refrain in the singing of the black slaves when they went to work. One launched the question, the other gave the response: here is a pattern that could somehow fix into the movement, into the march, a mechanism of organization of the discourse. But even this

---

* 'Go' and 'Call and respond' in English in the original.

does not correspond to the experience of the streets that I witnessed and studied in 2011. I participated a little in the Spanish movements in Spain; I studied closely the Brazilian movement of 2013 (a movement of extraordinary importance); and I am left with the uncertainty of not knowing how to define the new spatiality of the movements from a political point of view. But assuredly, since then, spatiality has become central. Black Lives Matter, Gilets Jaunes, and today's women's movements in Belarus – these are three very strong examples. Probably, then, it is worth keeping the metaphor and saying that we want to repeat the Commune in order to maintain a relationship between the council and the movement.

These difficulties do not take anything away from the imaginary of the Commune, even if – returning to the social struggles, in the spaces they occupy, and to Rimbaud, to the poetry I read before – while granting full respect to Kristin Ross, we must remember that the class struggle is also a struggle of mourning, ruptures, losses and death. I don't know whether you have ever been to Père-Lachaise, the cemetery of the Commune, where the execution wall and the mass graves can be seen. It is something that makes you want to cry when you go there; but this, too, has to be remembered: the class struggle is beautiful, but it is also a matter of life and death, and for the Commune it was so too. Lissagaray tells it well.

The planetary commune

> Let us try to frame the Commune as a political form, recalling other geographies and times in which the Commune has been recalled – I'm thinking in particular of the Commune of Shanghai and of that of Oaxaca. Even remaining with the Paris Commune, recent studies tend to trace a genealogy that is not attributable just to the city perimeter of Paris but broadens it within that constitutively transnational dimension in which political phenomena take place, and hence looks at the Parisian event also in a colonial–decolonial dimension of struggles that extend beyond the specific moment. But the Commune becomes, specifically, also a political dimension that does not reproduce itself as much as proposes itself as a political form. What does this reappearance of the Commune tell us, despite the obvious differences in contexts?

The Commune has had enormous significance in political thought precisely inasmuch as it has been treated as a political form. But every real political experience we live recalls it as an event, and often as a defeated event. So we have on the one hand the political model of the

Commune as a model of council-based activity, as direct democracy. And on the other we have the experience of a real political form, of a real political event, which is an event of defeat, of crude repression.

When I was young, I remember that, when I talked about the Commune with the old cadres of the Communist Party – and obviously I did so with the enthusiasm of a neophyte – they, deriding me, would remind me that the Commune had been defeated but its defeat had been largely redeemed by the triumph of the Russian Revolution and of the Red Army in the defence of Stalingrad and the conquest of Berlin... things that were far from derisory... and then there was China, and so on. One third of the world was included in this act of redemption. This triumphalist teleology soon proved itself to me to be false. More and more I found myself in need of going back to basics and building on the new experiences of struggle. Here the problem was to combine the ideal of the Paris Commune with that of Shanghai or Oaxaca and with the global reality in the history of proletarian revolutions. I think this would have been one of Marx's great problems, and in some ways it was, as can be seen from the publication of his researches in old age, especially the anthropological writings – or, to put it better, after *Capital*, when he began his anthropological studies and sought to find some continuity in community forms of organization between the past and the future. I have never been keen on these kinds of intellectual adventure, because I think that there is a logical impossibility in connecting a form of utopia, albeit a concrete utopia, to a historical path. I have the scepticism of an old-time materialist. But Marx was a materialist too, and yet he tried to find in the Russian *obscina*, as appears in the letters to Vera Zasulic, the possibility of determining a historical continuity of the communist model. As for Mao: he was against the Shanghai Commune, but he built communes in the mountains of Henan: a truly living and armed dual power, with its factories but also with its schools, in which communist cadres were produced by transforming illiterate peasants into the future leaders of the Chinese socialist state – and anyway by putting them through the exercise of arms. This was an extraordinary experience, one of the few that took place in a state of exception – I don't mean the constitutional exception, but the exceptional story of two Maoist wars, the civil war and the war against Japan, which are mutually interrelated. And here, in the middle, there is a first realization of a counterpower.

Now, these are the broader dimensions in which I believe the theoretical model of the common needs to be reproposed and adapted to reality. Otherwise I'm very afraid of utopias, of any utopia. When I look around, I see ethically and politically formidable experiences, the various ZADs [*zones à défendre*, zones to defend] and other spatialized experiences of class conflict. However, I do not believe that with this we are on an adequate terrain, at the level of the current needs of revolutionary thought. What is needed is to understand what it means to bring into being a dual power [*doppio potere*] that does not dissolve complexity but succeeds in preserving it, manages to overcome and use it, and at the same time destroys it; a power that does not nestle within the complexity of power but becomes a virus, which attacks the main nerve centres.

This in turn raises the problem of how the Commune can represent a political model and how it could have been valid, for example in experiences of decolonialization during the great struggles against colonialism. When you read, say, the work of Indian academics in subaltern studies,* Ranajit Guha in particular, you find descriptions of formidable experiences of class struggle in the wars of liberation against British colonialism in India. Whole states were involved in uprisings where millions and millions of people fought in ways that closely resembled those of the Commune.

But we should be careful. Today fortunately we have entered a postcolonial era. And I would not want to reiterate the illusion that this has created a smooth and unified world – an illusion to which I came very close in *Empire* – after the illusion that globalization has rendered this world homogeneous (the first, the second, the third). There are huge differences on all sides, it cannot be helped; but the unified global or imperial–global scope remains. Thus, if these differences exist, they must be understood at a single level. And what is needed at this level is not the discovery or rediscovery of old formulas or old experiences: not small utopias but rather a constituent imagination. The problem of power has to be addressed in its entirety – as they did in the Paris Commune.

So let us ask ourselves: how can a counterpower be constituted, or rather a practice of rupture that traverses and destroys the complexity of capitalist power? We are not talking here only about taking the state; what is to be destroyed is sovereignty, capitalist sovereignty. Unfortunately that's a different matter altogether. And this transition is something damn difficult, even from the point of view of imagining it; but it is nevertheless the terrain on which we must press to the

---

* 'subaltern studies' in English in the original.

limit our capacity for analysis and our experiences – with the certainty that every time you create a break on this link the whole chain breaks, every time you break that transition everything else collapses almost automatically, as it always does when something breaks under tension. Having said this, it is clear that all individual problems conglomerated in power (for instance the ecological problem is central today) have to be linked together in the destruction and transformation that take place in a prospective chain, in a single dispositif. This is what the Commune teaches us.

I always say this to my closest comrades: today we have to imagine a kind of Pinocchio and build him in such a way that he gradually acquires a sense of complexity – a bit like in seventeenth- and eighteenth-century fairytales where a flower was placed in front of a Pinocchietto, in order for us to imagine how smell could awake the other senses. Today the point is to experience not the senses but passions, common passions. We have to invent the cyborg of the common. We have to be capable of combining the postmodern – its economy, technology, social and cultural relationships, and everything in it – with the humanist passion of the Commune, of being together, of building together, in freedom and in equality.

The Commune today

A few last points. What can it mean to think of the present and of the political future through the lens of the Commune? I mean this in two senses. What can the Commune mean today politically and organizationally, as secession, separation of pieces of metropolis, of territory, of territoriality – what does it mean to think of this dimension of secession, of rupture, of parts... Earlier you mentioned the ZADs as an example of low-level micro-dynamics, as small pieces of territory in secession; but can we think of this dynamic of separation and of rupture at metropolitan level? As a counter-construction of other powers? Is this intuition of the Commune thinkable today? On the other side of the problem, how can the semantic area of the concatenation between Commune, commons, communism, common and community be anticipated, even in the light of experiences such as those of 2011 and 2013, or of the more recent ones in Chile and the United States, or again by looking at the Gilets Jaunes, with their spatiality made of expansive and widespread territoriality, their roundabouts that became molecular camps on French soil and then focused on the intensity of Saturdays, on the assaults on the metropolis ...?

Three things have made a great impression on me in recent years. One is Black Lives Matter, the second is the Gilets Jaunes movement, and the third, which I find amazing (also because I was lucky enough to have direct contact with it), is the women of Belarus. What's happening there is incredible: women, and only women, come and demonstrate every Sunday, filling the streets up to hundreds of thousands. These women have produced an irresistible political movement, while the policemen of power are exclusively male. This movement of women occurs in a country that is far from wretched and has succeeded in maintaining a considerable level of heavy and light industry, which is linked to Russia but has sufficient autonomy to be, for example, employed in Chinese style (and this also explains many of the anxieties of the West), as a subordinate workforce, by the large western pools.* These women demonstrate to demand a democratic transformation of the political order in a society with a traditionally good level of welfare, and obviously they already include in their struggle the defence and development of all their needs as women. It is a formidable thing – the first time a political movement consists entirely of women. I don't want to upset my women comrades, who will rightly observe that any movement of women (especially the ones we have recently witnessed here and in Latin America) is political; but this is a 'political' that looks directly at the common, at the state, and at the latter's radical transformation.

As for the American movements, nothing remains to say that has not been said already ... while there is no doubt that the Gilets Jaunes movement – for all the ambiguities it has gradually revealed (accompanied today, unfortunately, by an evident inability to bounce back) – has shown a very high level of perception and proposal of the common, and not simply as a recollection of the Commune (which is always there in France, in any subversive movement). And this is where we saw a perception and proposal of the common: in a strange moment, when it seemed that struggles were completely blocked and Macron's Republic had, so to speak, removed their plausibility, the Gilets Jaunes suddenly popped up, with their invention of a space of mobilization on Saturdays, on the day when people rest. A mobilization on the day of rest... The first few times when I saw them I asked myself: 'What are these people doing, are they going to Mass?' It really looked a bit like that. In short, the movement revealed something that decidedly surpassed any claim or possibility

---

* 'pools' in English in the original.

of being reduced to a liturgical fact; it became a permanent invention, because this coming together turned out to be (and I think this applies to the Commune in general) a real forge of powers [*potenze*], a moment of formidable expression. To succeed in getting together in a society where everyone said that politics was finished, that politics was dead... what nonsense! What we saw was an exceptional bottom-up politicization. It was a coming together and a marching on Saturday afternoons, and this gave rise to a road map in which all the complexity of capitalist domination was picked through, one page after another, as in plucking a daisy. This was the first communard aspect, the analytical Commune.

The second communard element in the Gilets Jaunes was that, as a partial and open engine of subversion, this movement brought about the convergence of all other forces – remarkably, even of the trade unions... always jealous of their corporate interests (but less so today and more often in defence of their very survival, because precisely that corporate aspect has reduced them to being a simple expression or sub-expression of the power of the state). The Gilets Jaunes succeeded in awakening the corporate trade union forces too, and invited them to moments of convergence of struggle, but above all they produced a new discovery of the terrain of struggle, the struggle over the common. What are in fact the proposals of the Gilets Jaunes? They are referendum – not at all in the style of the Five Star movement, but one that means 'we want to intervene in the legislative process directly'; and, second, we want to decide on public spending, on the tax–wage relationship, and on the *redistribution of income*. This last element, economic–salarial, is an essential one that corresponds to another, democratic – so that one cannot be without the other. You cannot ask for absolute, direct democracy if you do not ask for equal wages distributed to all. The Commune again?

Final problem: we live in a society in which the mechanism of production brings about a profound cooperation of living labour, and proposes a common ontology of work. The question is how to make this ontology speak. The political model that the Paris Commune produced came before the emergence of the common as a power of production; we are probably instead in a situation where that productive power of the common precedes, has consolidated, and is our environment. This should represent an anthropological privilege. But capital has appropriated it. And yet the common as an anthropological privilege is by now implanted in our nature and can become explosive. It is clear that, if we succeed in expressing it, everything blows up. And we have to be very careful with that, because we must always remember what Lissagaray said about the class struggle... even in the face of just one single rupture, capital responds with all its forces. Capital is bad, and I don't say it lightly. It knows that it must destroy one to prevent many, too many, from destroying it. So long live the common, and may it bring us good!

Notes

Notes to Chapter 1

1 Ian Gough, 'State spending in advanced capitalism', *New Left Review*, 92 (1975), p. 53.
2 See the controversy opened by S. von Flatow and F. Huisken's 'Zum Problem der Ableitung des bürgerlichen Staates', *Probleme des Klassenkampfs*, 7 (May 1973) and pursued by H. Reichelt, 'Einige Ammerkungen Flatows von und zu S. F. Huiskens Aufsatz...', *Gesellschaft: Beiträge zur Marxschen Theorie*, 1 (1974), pp. 12–30; H. Hochberger, 'Probleme einer materialistischen Bestimmung des Staates', *Gesellschaft: Beiträge zur Marxschen Theorie*, 2 (1974), pp. 155–203; H. Gerstenberger, 'Klassenantagonismus, Konkurrenz und Staatsfunktionen', *Gesellschaft: Beiträge zur Marxschen Theorie*, 3 (1975), pp. 7–26. Other recent contributions can be found in these articles' bibliographies, which I have not consulted so far.
3 Jim O'Connor, *The Fiscal Crisis of the State*, New York: St Martin's Press, 1973.
4 Karl Marx, *Capital*, vol. 2, London: Penguin/New Left Review, 1992, chs 20–1.
5 Gough, 'State spending', p. 57.
6 Following in Mandel's footsteps, see D. Yaffe, 'The crisis of profitability', *New Left Review*, 80 (1973), and D. Yaffe, 'The Marxian theory of crisis, capital and state', *Conference of Socialist Economists Bulletin* (hereafter *CSEB*), winter 1972. It seems that J. Kirsch, 'Zur Analyse des politischen Systems', *Gesellschaft*, 1 (1974), pp. 78–131, but esp. 95 and 97, also falls into such ambiguities.
7 Karl Marx, *Grundrisse der Kritik der Politischen Ökonomie* [*Foundations of a Critique of Political Economy*], translated here from the Italian edition, vol. 2, Florence: La Nuova Italia, 1970, p. 60. [Given the nature of the material, all subsequent references to Marx will be to Italian translations,

which are also the source of the English versions presented in this chapter.]
8 Friedrich Engels, *Antidühring*, translated here from the Italian edition, Rome: Editori Riuniti, 1950, p. 303.
9 Rosa Luxemburg, *Ausgewählte Reden und Schrijnen*, translated here from the Italian edition: Rosa Luxenburg, *Scritti politici*, vol. 1, Rome: Editori Internazionali Riuniti, 2012, p. 720.
10 Marx, *Grundrisse*, vol. 2, pp. 396ff. It should be noted that observations and reservations were raised to the interpretation given by Roman Rosdolsky, especially to the concept of 'overall capital' [*capitale complessivo*], in his fundamental *The Making of Marx's* Capital, London: Pluto, 1977; and they came from all sides. See particularly W. Schwarz, 'Das "Kapital im allgemeinen" und die "Konkurrenz" im ökonomischen Werk von Karl Marx', *Gesellschaft*, 1 (1974), pp. 222–47 – which remains the most important contribution. In this instance, Rosdolsky is seen as having confounded several levels of the scientific abstraction operated by Marx, confusing the level of total capital (a mere logical category) with that on which competition operates, a category that is not logical but historical and historically effective. It is obviously necessary that the studies on the *Grundrisse* should proceed to an entire reverification of Marx's argument here, and there is no doubt that some passages in Rosdolsky need to be revised – but certainly not, in my opinion, those relating to the concept of overall capital, which is fundamental to Marx's thought and is explained by Rosdolsky as the tendential category that begins to approach its actuality today. On the other hand, in Marx the relationship between logical categories and historical categories seems a little more complex than in Schwarz's definition of it.
11 For documentation concerning the most significant examples of public spending and welfare policy in the United States and of the workers' struggle in this area, see especially the articles of P. Carpignano, 'Note su classe operaia e capitale in America negli anni Sessanta', in S. Bologna, P. Carpignano and A. Negri, *Crisi e organizzazione operaia*, Milan: Feltrinelli, 1974, pp. 73–98, and P. Carpignano, 'Disoccupazione made in USA', *Sociological Criticism*, 35 (1975), pp. 115–28. The literature on this question is starting to be extensive in English-speaking countries, and I think that it is likely to multiply very soon, given the problems raised by the impending bankruptcy of New York City Hall.
12 On these problems in general, see again O'Connor, *The Fiscal Crisis of the State*, esp. p. 9 and the last chapters. For Italy, from a point of view of a critique and rationalization written from within the system, see F. Reviglio, 'La crisi della finanza pubblica (1970–1974): indicazioni per una diagnosi e una terapia', *Rivista di diritto finanziario*, 1 (1975), n.p.
13 O'Connor, *The Fiscal Crisis of the State*, p. 7.
14 In the distinctions he makes, O'Connor is probably inspired by Claus Offe's analysis of the political structures of the state. For an in-depth

view of Offe's work on these questions, see particularly Claus Offe, *Strukturprobleme des kapitalistischen Staates*, Frankfurt: Suhrkamp, 1972, esp. pp. 27ff. and 123ff, and Claus Offe, 'Krisen des Krisenmanagement: Elemente einer politischen Krisentheorie', in M. Jänicke, ed., *Herrschaft und Krise*, Opladen: Westdeutscher Verlag, 1973, pp. 192–223, esp. 116ff.

15 Gough, 'State spending', p. 71, note.
16 Joachim Hirsch, *Wissenschaftlich-technischer Fortschritt und politisches System*, Frankfurt: Suhrkamp, 1970, pp. 87, 91, 93.
17 Yaffe, 'Crisis of profitability', p. 52.
18 See esp. Marx, *Capital*, in the Italian edition, Rome: Rinascita, 1954: vol. 2, pp. 64–70, and also vol. 1, pp. 38–9. See the whole ch. 3 in vol. 1.
19 Marx's definition of productive work runs throughout his mature work, with a notable coherence of emphasis. See Marx, *Grundrisse*, vol. 1, pp. 244–54, 261–2, 274–5, 277–8, 279–82, 291–2, 294–8, 317–18, 336–9, 363–70 and vol. 2, pp. 84, 384, 397–415, 456–7, 461–3, 483, 555, 575–7, 648–54; Marx, *Capital*, esp. vol. 1, ch. 2, pp. 221–2; Karl Marx, *Unpublished Chapter VI*, in the Italian edition: Florence: La Nuova Italia, 1969, pp. 57–8, 73–94; Karl Marx, *Theories of Surplus Value*, in the Italian edition: Rome: Editori Riuniti, 1961, pp. 269–470, 585–613. But later on Marx's thought on productive labour ended in very reductive positions among his followers (his definition of it was charged with class struggle intentionality; see Friedrich Behrens, *Produktive Arbeit und technische Intelligenz*, a self-published study from 1970). There is not much help for proceeding in the debate in the article by E. Altvater and F. Huisken, 'Produktive und unproduktive Arbeit als Kampfbegriffe, als Kategorien zur Analyse der Klassenverhaltnisse und der Reproduktionsbedingungen des Kapitals', *Sozialistische Politik*, 8 (1970), pp. 47–92 (http://www.elmaraltvater.net/articles/Altvater_Articl e1a.pdf), translated into Italian in 1975 as a book, under the title *Lavoro produttivo e improduttivo*.
20 Marx, *Capital*, vol. 1, ch. 2, pp. 221–2.
21 See Ian Gough, 'Marx's theory of productive and unproductive labour', *New Left Review*, 76 (1972), pp. 47–72; John Harrison, 'Productive and unproductive labour in Marx's political economy', *CSEB*, 2.6 (1973), pp. 70–82; B. Fine, 'A note on productive and unproductive labour', *CSEB*, 2.6 (1973), pp. 99–102; Paul Bullock, 'Categories of labour power for capital', *CSEB*, 2.6 (1973), pp. 82–99; Paul Bullock, 'Defining productive labour for capital', *CSEB*, 2.9 (1974)), pp. 15–29.
22 Gough, 'State spending in advanced capitalism', p. 83.
23 Bob Rowthorn, 'Skilled labour in the Marxist system', *CSEB*, 1 (1974), pp. 25–45, here p. 36.
24 See Marx's research and conclusions on public debt in primitive accumulation.
25 A particularly interesting point in the aforementioned discussion

among British economists concerns the extension of the concept of productive labour to domestic work. See John Harrison, 'The political economy of housework', *CSEB*, 3 (1973), pp. 35–51; Ian Gough and John Harrison, 'Unproductive labour and housework again', *CSEB*, 4.1 (1975), pp. 69–75. All these issues are available at https://journals.sagepub.com/page/cnc/collections/bulletin.

26 We are awaiting an article on this subject by Luciano Ferrari Bravo that should soon appear in *Aut Aut* and should offer a useful philological approach to developing an analysis of the insufficiency (and tendentiousness) of Marx's definitions of productive and unproductive labour.

27 The fragment on machines in Marx, *Grundrisse*, vol. 2, from p. 388 on.

28 Marx, *Capital*, vol. 1, ch. 2, pp. 215–16 (conclusion of the discussion on the factory legislation).

29 See the conclusions in Rosdolsky, *The Making of Marx's Capital*, pp. 342 ff.

30 E.g. F. Galgano, *Le istituzioni dell'economia capitalistica*, Bologna: Zanichelli, 1974, esp. pp. 33–8.

31 R. Guastini, in his review of Galgano, disputes – in my opinion, in ways that are too hasty and traditional – a certain analytical correctness of the approach of the author under consideration. See R. Guastini, 'Stato del capitale e neotogliattismo', *Sociologia del diritto*, 1 (1975), pp. 143–4.

32 Marx, *Capital*, esp. vol. 1, ch. 2; also more specifically vol. 3, ch. 2 (pp. 74–5 and 154–5).

33 But see esp. the analysis in Elmar Altvater, 'Notes on some problems of state interventionism', *Kapitalistate*, 1 (1973), pp. 96–108; 2 (1973), pp. 76–83. https://www.marxists.org/subject/economy/authors/altvater/1972/probsstate.htm.

34 Marx, *Capital*, vol. 3, ch. 1, pp. 285–95 and 296–324.

35 Hirsch, *Wissenschaftlich-technischer Fortschritt*, stresses very well and with great appropriateness the continuing inherence of socialization processes in the structure of the contemporary state (see in particular pp. 89, 91, 93, 103). On this line see also the recent contribution of J. Agnoli, *Überlegungen zum bürgerlichen Staat*, Berlin: Wagenbach, 1975, in particular the chapter 'Der Staat des Kapitals'.

36 Wolf-Dieter Narr and Claus Offe, eds, *Wohlfahrtsstaat und Massenloyalität*, Cologne: Kiepenheuer & Witsch, 1975 is a useful contribution, summarizing and partly didactic, on the difficulties faced in this area by state administration. J. Esser, *Einführung in die materialistische Staatsanalyse*, Frankfurt: Campus Verlag, 1975 brings a balanced view on the criticism of Offe's sociological and structuralist objectivism and a proper assessment of the merits of *Krisentheorie* in comparison with other positions in the German environment.

37 The reference is again to Marx, *Grundrisse*, vol. 2 (the fragment on machines).

38 On this subject, see essentially Rowthorn, 'Skilled labour'.
39 A. Negri, *Crisi dello stato-piano*, Milan: Feltrinelli, 1974; see also A. Negri, 'Partito operaio contro il lavoro', in S. Bologna, P. Carpignano and A. Negri, *Crisi e organizzazione operaia*, Milan: Feltrinelli, 1974, pp. 99–160.
40 The attempt to relate the fundamental problems of political science and planning science back to the fundamental antagonisms of the socialization of production is very clear in Hirsch, *Wissenschaftlich-technischer Fortschritt*, passim (esp. pp. 85 and 128).
41 On this 'negative' conscience, see particularly the texts of the so-called *Planungsdiskussion* ('joint discussion') that developed in Western Germany around the 1970s. Bibliography can be found in Hirsch, *Wissenschaftlich-technischer Fortschritt*, pp. 80, 93–4.
42 Rosdolsky, *The Making of Marx's* Capital, pp. 330–64.
43 Mediobanca, ed., *La finanza pubblica, 1968–72*, 2 vols, Milan: Mediobanca, 1974.
44 See again Reviglio, 'La crisi della finanza pubblica'. Some of the considerations that follow come from this study.
45 The latest testimony is a bitter one: Giorgio Ruffolo, *Riforme e controriforme*, Bari: Laterza, 1975.
46 M. Paci, *Mercato del lavoro e classi sociali in Italia*, Bologna: Il Mulino, 1973.
47 For an in-depth study of this topic, see A. Negri, *Proletari e Stato*, Milan: Feltrinelli, 1976 – a booklet published in the Opuscoli Marxisti series.
48 Reviglio, 'La crisi della finanza pubblica', pp. 177–8.
49 See for example the documentation regarding Germany in H. J. Weissbach, *Planungswissenschaft: Eine Analyze der Entwicklungsbedingungen und Entwicklungsformen der Arbeitsmarkt – und Berufsforschung*, Giessen: Achenbach, 1975.
50 J. Agnoli and P. Bruckner, *Die Transformation der Demokratie*, Frankfurt: Europäische Verlagsanstalt, 1968), a book no longer new, was completely prescient regarding this development. On the reorientation of political science and the practices of power in this area, see Narr and Offe, *Wohlfahrtsstaat und Massenloyalität*, with references.
51 See N. Bobbio, 'Intorno all'analisi funzionale del diritto', *Sociologia del diritto*, 1 (1975), n.p.
52 Concerning Germany, I refer here mainly to the work of Niklas Luhmann (see A. Febbraio, 'Sociologia del diritto e funzionalismo strutturale nell'opera di N. Luhmann', *Sociologia del diritto*, 2 (1974), n.p.). As for the United States, a reference to the work of James Willard Hurst seems apposite here; see E. Lombardi, 'La logica dell'esperienza di J. Willard Hurst', *Materiali per una storia della cultura giuridica*, 2 (1972), pp. 519–86.
53 But the communists are challenged to prove themselves (albeit with many ambiguities) regarding this 'heterogony of ends'; see J. Seifert, *Kampf*

um Verfassungspositionen: Materialien über Grenzen und Möglichkeiten von Rechtspolitik, Cologne: Europäische Verlagsanstalt, 1974.

54 A piece of research useful in this respect seems to me T. Krämer-Bordoni et al., *Die Kommune in der Staatsorganization*, Frankfurt: Suhrkamp, 1974. This volume, put together by a team of young authors, contains an important piece, with a somewhat rigid but critical content, which argues against Offe's theory of crisis: T. Kramer-Badoni, 'Krise und Krisenpotential im Spätkapitalismus', pp. 115–30.

55 A reference to the dramatic pages written in the 1930s by F. Neumann on the democratic state and on the authoritarian state is indispensable here. No less interesting are the notes and analyses offered around these same themes in A. Sohn-Rethel, *Ökonomie und Klassenstruktur des deutschen Faschismus*, Frankfurt: Suhrkamp, 1973 (with a preface by J. Agnoli, B. Blanke and N. Kadritzke).

56 Marx, *Grundrisse*, vol. 2, pp. 409–11 (again, all passages are translated here from the Italian).

57 On these questions, and esp. on the reconstruction of class composition and on the dialectic of needs, I refer again to Negri, *Proletari e stato*.

58 See R. Theobald, ed., *The Guaranteed Income*, Garden City, NY: Doubleday, 1966.

59 J. H. Goldthorpe et al., *The Affluent Worker*, 3 vols., Cambridge: Cambridge University Press, 1968–9 is fundamental in this regard. See also W. G. Runcinam, *Relative Deprivation and Social Justice*, Harmondsworth: Penguin, 1972.

60 One could think here of Oskar Negt – of his works on education and on working-class consciousness in a technological society, as well as of the mass of ideology produced around the '150 hours' programme. [This was a well-known achievement of worker education in Italy in the 1970s.]

61 Interestingly, there has been a recent reprise of the topic of class composition by German authors. See in particular C. Eckart et al., 'Arbeiterbewusstsein, Klassenzusammensetzung und Ökonomische Entwicklung: Empirische Thesen zum instrumentellen Bewusstsein', *Gesellschaft*, 4 (1975), pp. 7–64.

62 Some hints about this can be found in Claus Offe, *Leistungsprinzip und industrielle Arbeit*, Frankfurt: Europäische Verlagsanstalt, 1970 (see esp. the Introduction).

63 Finally, on these questions, see U. Rödel, *Forschungsprioritäten und technologische Entwicklung*, Frankfurt: Suhrkamp, 1972; Carl Rolshausen, *Wissenschaft und gesellschaftliche Reproduktion*, Frankfurt: Suhrkamp, 1975; and J. H. Mendner, *Technologische Entwicklung und Arbeitsprozess*, Frankfurt: Fischer, 1975.

64 M. Cacciari, 'Lavoro, valorizzazione e "cervello sociale"', *Aut Aut*, 145–6 (1975), pp. 3–40.

65 R. Alquati, *Sindacato e partito*, Turin: Edizioni Stampatori, 1974, p. 165.

66 See B. Wahrenkamp, ed., *Technologie und Kapital*, Frankfurt: Suhrkamp,

Notes to pp. 24–28　　　　　　　　　　　　　　　　　　　185

1973 (esp. A. Sohn-Rethel's chapter 'Technische Intelligenz zwischen Kapitalismus und Sozialismus').
67 Alquati, *Sindacato e partito*, pp. 165–6.
68 I should say here that when I speak of productive potential I don't mean Sweezy and Baran's notion of surplus, as configured in underconsumerism theory. My notion is quite opposite to theirs. The question I ask in the text came to me when I reread an old typescript by Ferruccio Gambino (from 1970, I think), entitled 'Forza invenzione e forza-lavoro: ipotesi'. This essay ends by defining a project that seems to me of great interest and on which there is still work to be done: 'The so-called productive potential that presides over Sweezy and Baran's notion of surplus has to be included in the capacity (still to be built) of the working class to dominate social knowledge as a whole: to dominate it endemically, down to the elimination of political mediations.' This is precisely the question, and today we are beginning to approach it.
69 For a definition of the planning model, which takes into account the terms of political science, see S. S. Cohen, *Modern Capitalist Planning: The French Model*, Berkeley: University of California Press, 1977. The discussion of this model in H. G. Haupt and S. Leibfried, 'Planung im Kapitalismus: das französische Modell', *Leviathan*, 2 (1974), pp. 313–22 contains a large critical bibliography on planning.
70 On this question it is perhaps useful to recall the fundamental contributions of N. Kaldor, *Causes of the Slow Rate of Economic Growth of the UK: An Inaugural Lecture*, London: Cambridge University Press, 1966, and M. Morishima, *Marx's Economics: A Dual Theory of Value and Growth*, Cambridge: Cambridge University Press, 1973.
71 On this theme, it is sufficient to see the pathetic proposals of the Cambridge Political Economy Group and Claus Koch, 'England Krise: Ursachen und Abhilfen', *Leviathan*, 3.3 (1975), pp. 338–69 (the article came to my attention in this German translation).
72 See the arguments and the reconstruction of Marx's thinking in the Epilogue to Rosdolsky, *The Making of Marx's Capital*.
73 See R. Damus, *Wertkategorien als Mittel der Planung: Zur Widersprüchlichkeit der Planung gesamtgesellschaftlicher Prozesse in der DDR*, Erlangen: Politladen, 1973. But one can deduce – at least from the news of working-class and proletarian struggles in the Soviet Union that began to filter through – that enforced control must occur even in the USSR planning process. See, among others, M. Holubenko, 'The Soviet working class: Discontent and opposition', *Critique*, 4 (1975), pp. 5–25.
74 See e.g. H. Haussermann, 'Die administrative Organization als Problem politischer Innovation', *Leviathan*, 2 (1974), pp. 23–62 (a piece I came upon recently).
75 For contributions on these issues, see Claus Offe, 'Rationalitätskriterien und Funktionsprobleme politisch-administrativen Handelns', *Leviathan* 3 (1974), pp. 333–46; G. Schmid and D. Freiburghaus, 'Techniken

politischer Planung: vom Mertkalkul zum Plankalkul?', *Leviathan*, 3 (1974), pp. 346–82; W. Ehlert, 'Politische Planung: und was davon übrig bleibt', *Leviathan*, 1 (1975), pp. 84–114; V. Ronge, 'Entpolitisierung der Forschungspolitik', *Leviathan*, 3 (1975), pp. 307–37.

76 F. Gerstenberger, 'Produktion und Qualifikation', *Leviathan*, 2 (1975), pp. 251–79.

77 Carpignano, 'Disoccupazione, made in USA' reports some very effective statements of American leaders on the impossibility of proceeding in this direction.

78 The wealth of the dual labour market is not new, but enjoyed an innovation in the 1970s, when it became an active part of labour policy – that is, of the segmentation of the labour market. See Michael J. Piore and Peter B. Doeringer, 'Unemployment and the dual labour market', *Public Interest*, 38 (1975), pp. 67–79; D. Freiburghaus and G. Schmid, 'Theorie der Segmentierung von Arbeitsitsmarkten', *Leviathan*, 3 (1975), pp. 417–48.

79 In Claus Offe, *Berufsbildungsreform: Eine Fallstudie über Reformpolitik*, Frankfurt: Suhrkamp, 1975, the author's structuralistic conception and class tension seem to reach a new level of equilibrium, in which the moments of antagonism typical of the socialization processes can occur more insistently.

80 Norberto Bobbio, 'Gramsci e la concezione della società civile', in *Studi gramsciani: Atti del convegno tenuto a Roma nei giorni 11–13 gennaio 1958*, Rome: Editori Riuniti, 1958, pp. 73–86. (Republished a few times, e.g. in Norberto Bobbo, *Gramsci e la concezione della società civile*, Milan: Feltrinelli, 1976, pp. 17–43, and now also available at https://marioxmancini.medium.com/gramsci-e-la-concezione-della-società-civile-defcbb4e216a).

81 One can find an analysis of the situation in Germany in Karl H. Roth, *L' 'altro' movimento operaio*, Milan: Feltrinelli, 1976 and in C. T. Bolbrinker, *Klassenanalyse als Organizationsfrage*, Giessen: Focus Verlag, 1975.

82 Alfred Sohn-Rethel, *Die ökonomische Doppelnatur des Spätkapitalismus, Luchterhand*, Darmstad: Hermann Luchterhand Verlag, 1972. See also Sohn-Rethel, 'Technische Intelligenz' and, for the remarkable contribution they bring to the present discussion, Alfred Sohn-Rethel, *Warenform und Denkform, Aufsätze*, Vienna: Europe Verlag, 1971; Alfred Sohn-Rethel, *Geistige und korperliche Arbeit* (2nd edn), Frankfurt: Suhrkamp, 1972; and Alfred Sohn-Rethel, *Materialistische Erkenntnistheorie und Vergesellschaftung der Arbeit*, Berlin: Merve Verlag, 1971.

83 Rosdolsky, *The Making of Marx's Capital*, p. 490. Again, see the fragment on machines in Marx, *Grundrisse*, vol. 2.

84 The reference is to 'Private and communal property', in Karl Marx, *1844 Manuscripts*, Moscow: Progress Publishers, 1959, and to 'Communism', in Karl Marx and Friedrich Engels, *The German Ideology*, edited by C. J. Arthur, London: Lawrence & Wishart, 1970.

85 It is clear that when I talk of a necessary openness of scientific interest to

criticism against politics – understood as a development of the critique of political economy, at the current level of development of the class struggle – I mean essentially an analysis that moves at two levels. The first level is that of the critique of the everyday; the second level is that of the critique of administration, in which institutional political forces are necessarily included. In my judgement, addressing this second level has nothing to do with the chatter about what is called 'the autonomy of the political'; on the contrary, carrying out today a critical analysis of politics in Marxian terms means developing a critique of political economy in its own right and removing any residual autonomy (however relevant) from the state and from all those who participate in the organization of capitalist exploitation, starting from the state.

86 A 'strategic dimension of the refusal' and a 'tactical dimension of abnormal usages' are, on the other hand, indications that have circulated for some time among scientific researchers and employees in research establishments, in work that indirectly produces surplus value.

Notes to Chapter 4

1 For a critical review of the political economy of the common, see Carlo Vercellone et al., *Managing the Commons in the Knowledge Economy*. Report D3.2, D-CENT (Decentralized Citizens ENgagement Technologies). European Project 2015. May 2015. http://dcentproject.eu/wp-content/uploads/2015/07/D3.2-complete-ENG-v2.pdf.
2 See Sandro Chignola, 'Vita lavoro linguaggi: Biopolitica e biocapitalismo, *EuroNomade*, 12 October 2015.
3 See Laurent de Sutter, ed., *Accélérations*, Paris: PUF, 2016.

Notes to Chapter 6

1 Daniel J. Elazar, *Exploring Federalism*, Tuscaloosa: University of Alabama Press, 1987.

Notes to Chapter 7

1 Karl Marx, *Über Friedrich Lists Buch* Das nationale System der politischen Ökonomie, Paris: Études et Documentation Internationales, 1975 [1845]. Translated here from the Italian.
2 C. B. Macpherson, *The Political Theory of Possessive Individualism: Hobbes to Locke*, Oxford: Oxford University Press, 2011.
3 Thomas Hobbes, *Leviathan* 10.16.
4 Manuel Castells and Robert Castel, *Les métamorphoses de la question sociale: une chronique du salariat*, Paris: Fayard, 1995 (also Paris: Folio-Gallimard, 2000); Manuel Castells, *The Rise of the Network Society*, Oxford: Wiley Blackwell, 2009.

5 Luc Boltanski and Eve Chiappello, *Le nouvel esprit du capitalisme*, Paris: Gallimard, 1999.
6 André Orléan, *L'empire de la valeur*, Paris: Seuil, 2011; Christian Marazzi, *E il denaro va*, Milan: Bollati Boringhieri, 1998.
7 Gunnar Heinsohn and Otto Steiger, 'The property theory of interest and money', in J. Smithin, ed., *What Is Money?* London: Routledge, 2000, pp. 67–100.
8 Jean-Marie Harribey, book review of André Orléan, *L'empire de la valeur*, *Revue de la Régulation*, 10 (2011). http://regulation.revues.org/9483.
9 Rosa Luxemburg, 'Introduction to political economy', in *The Complete Works of Rosa Luxemburg*, vol. 1, London: Verso, 2013, p. 286.
10 Heinsohn and Steiger, 'Property theory of interest and money'; Harribey, book review.
11 See Antonio Negri, 'Rileggendo Pašukanis: note di discussione', in his *La forma stato*, Milan: Feltrinelli, 1977, pp. 161–95.

Notes to Chapter 8

1 Étienne Tassin, *Un monde commun*, Paris: Seuil, 2003.
2 Saskia Sassen, *Expulsions*, Cambridge, MA: Harvard University Press, 2014.
3 Franck Fischbach, *Le sens du social: La puissance de la cooperation*, Montréal: Lux, 2015.
4 I picked this formula from the title of Didier Fassin's beautiful new book: *La raison humanitaire: une histoire morale du temps présent*, Paris: Seuil/Gallimard, 2010.

Notes to Chapter 10

1 Michael Hardt and Antonio Negri, *Commonwealth*, Cambridge, MA: Harvard University Press, 2009. For subsequent references to this work, pagination is provided in the main text.
2 Michel Foucault, *Le courage de la vérité*, vol. 2: *Le gouvernement de soi et des autres*, Paris: Gallimard/Seuil, 2009. A different version of these lectures, delivered at the University of California, Berkeley in 1983, can be found in Michel Foucault, *Fearless Speech*, edited by Joseph Pearson, Los Angeles: Semiotext[e], 2001.
3 See e.g. Louis Althusser, *Lenin and Philosophy and Other Essays*, translated by Ben Brewster, New York: Monthly Review Press, 1971, p. 56.
4 Branden W. Joseph, 'Interview with Paolo Virno', translated by Alessia Ricciardi, *Grey Room*, 21 (2005), p. 34.
5 Antonio Negri, *Political Descartes*, translated by Matteo Mandarini and Alberto Toscano, London: Verso, 2007.
6 Carlo Levi, *Il futuro ha un cuore antico*, Turin: Einaudi, 1956.
7 Karl Heinz Roth, *Die 'andere' Arbeiterbewegung und die Entwicklung der*

kapitalistischen Repression von 1880 bis zur Gegenwart, Munich: Trikont Verlag, 1974. This book was widely discussed in the Italian extraparliamentary left in the mid-1970s.

8 Daniel Cohen, *Globalization and Its Enemies*, translated by Jessica B. Baker, Cambridge, MA: MIT Press, 2006; Antonio Negri, *Marx beyond Marx*, translated by Harry Cleaver, Michael Ryan and Maurizio Viano, New York: Autonomedia/Pluto, 1991. *Marx beyond Marx* is the published form of nine lectures given at the École normale supérieure in 1978. Cohen was a student there from 1973 to 1976.

9 Michel Foucault, 'Truth and juridical forms', in *The Essential Works of Foucault, 1954–1984*, vol. 3: *Power*, edited by James D. Faubion, New York: New Press, 2000, p. 7.

10 See e.g. the essays collected in Andrea Fumagelli and Sandro Mezzadra, eds, *Crisis in the Global Economy: Financial Markets, Social Struggles, and New Political Scenarios*, Los Angeles: Semiotext[e], 2010. Included in this collection is Carlo Vercellone's essay 'The crisis of the law of value and the becoming-rent of profit', whose argument forms an important point of reference in the third chapter of *Commonwealth*.

11 Christian Marazzi, *The Violence of Financial Capital*, translated by Kristina Lebedeva, Los Angeles: Semiotext[e], 2009.